Praise for

Dog Man

"Only a handful of visitors have tried to approach [Japan] through sympathetic imagination and not through surfaces or statistics, let alone analysis. Now, to that very small number, can be added Martha Sherrill, one of the most open and responsive writers around, whose special gift is for entering other lives so deeply that we feel their longings, their confinements, as our own. By the end of *Dog Man*, as Morie and Kitako pass through their eighties, we have come to know, and feel, their lives so fully that even the smallest detail . . . can bring tears. Sherrill somehow extends the story so deeply that it seems to stand for choices in all our lives."

—*The Washington Post*

"A rich compendium of fine nature writing. The scenes of men and their Akitas hunting black bears in Japan's northern mountains are thrilling."   —*The New York Times*

"*Dog Man* is a peerless tale of a life's work unfolding, written in prose so spare, rare, and beautiful it took my breath away. Morie Sawataishi's story, viewed through Martha Sherrill's compassionate gaze, is neither simple nor perfect, but rather an endlessly fascinating account of the obligations and joys of a life devoted to dogs. Written with equal parts rigor and grace, *Dog Man* captures something near the knotty essence of the human bond with dogs."   —David Wroblewski,

author of *The Story of Edgar Sawtelle*

"The story of Morie Sawataishi and his magnificent dogs—with their superior intelligence, stamina, fearlessness, and almost spiritual calm—is really about the search for enduring values and the determination to live life on one's own terms."

—Cathleen McGuigan, *Newsweek*

"A fascinating slice of cultural history, a chronicle of how one man stood against convention to pursue his own peculiar path."   —Elizabeth Mehren, *Los Angeles Times*

"The effect is of a first-rate novel, a character study whose central conflict is between man and a goal that is largely unattainable, a man who has lived his life as both selfish (in the immediate sense) and selfless (in the largest sense). He would probably be irritated by the term, but Morie Sawaitashi has lived an artist's life. Sherrill's continually fascinating book is a moving but never sentimental tribute to a man who is a throwback to the emotional fierceness of a samurai nation."   —*Palm Beach Post*

continued . . .

"Here's a story of a rare life lived in sharp contrast with the natural world—not just mountain and forest, but even more with that most interesting of species, the dog. These Akitas have wildness in them, enough to bring it out in those who look into their eyes. There's not a sentimental word in this book, but it will move you strongly."
—Bill McKibben,
author of *The End of Nature*

"The book brims with colorful characters, both human and canine. . . . Sherrill imbues [the] traditional Japanese lifestyle with dignity, and Morie's adventures should be enjoyed by dog lovers, breeders, and trainers."
—*Publishers Weekly*

"Sherrill offers great insight not only into one man and his dogs, but into an older, rural way of life unfamiliar to Westerners for whom Japan symbolizes fast-paced urban life and the latest technology."
—*Library Journal*

"*Dog Man* is an elegantly written account of a stubborn man who found meaning in old-fashioned values while his nation threw itself headlong into building an affluent, materialist, consumer-oriented society. In her wonderful journey to Japan's snow country, Martha Sherrill introduces us to a world—and a gruffly independent personality—that transcends national boundaries."
—John W. Dower,
author of *Embracing Defeat*

"A story of a hard life and dedication to preserving a traditional dog breed in the mountains of Japan. Fascinating descriptions of life in rural Japan during World War II."
—Temple Grandin,
author of *Animals in Translation*

"A moving portrait of the bond between dogs and breeder. At the end of the book, readers will have certainly learned a lot about Akitas, family dynamics, [and] Northern Japan after the war."
—The Associated Press

"*Dog Man* evokes the ancient myths: deep and quiet like high mountains in snow. Morie Sawataishi has learned from his beloved Akitas to embrace the wild. Read this book and feel that power."
—Neenah Ellis,
author of *If I Live to be 100*

Dog Man

An Uncommon Life
on a Faraway Mountain

Martha Sherrill

Riverhead Books
New York

RIVERHEAD BOOKS
Published by the Penguin Group
Penguin Group (USA) Inc.
375 Hudson Street, New York, New York 10014, USA
Penguin Group (Canada), 90 Eglinton Avenue East, Suite 700, Toronto, Ontario M4P 2Y3, Canada
(a division of Pearson Penguin Canada Inc.)
Penguin Books Ltd., 80 Strand, London WC2R 0RL, England
Penguin Group Ireland, 25 St. Stephen's Green, Dublin 2, Ireland (a division of Penguin Books Ltd.)
Penguin Group (Australia), 250 Camberwell Road, Camberwell, Victoria 3124, Australia
(a division of Pearson Australia Group Pty. Ltd.)
Penguin Books India Pvt. Ltd., 11 Community Centre, Panchsheel Park, New Delhi—110 017, India
Penguin Group (NZ), 67 Apollo Drive, Rosedale, North Shore 0632, New Zealand
(a division of Pearson New Zealand Ltd.)
Penguin Books (South Africa) (Pty.) Ltd., 24 Sturdee Avenue, Rosebank, Johannesburg 2196, South Africa

Penguin Books Ltd., Registered Offices: 80 Strand, London WC2R 0RL, England

Interior photo credits: Page 6: Courtesy of Perkins School for the Blind; Page 16: Mitsuro Aoyagi; Page 19 and 229: Courtesy of the author; Page 63: Aiken-no-Tomo Dog Magazine; All other photographs courtesy of the Sawataishi family.

Copyright © 2008 Martha Sherrill
Book design by Meighan Cavanaugh

The Penguin Press hardcover edition: March 2008
Riverhead trade paperback edition: August 2009
Riverhead trade paperback ISBN: 978-1-59448-390-5

The Library of Congress has catalogued The Penguin Press hardcover edition as follows:

Sherrill, Martha.
    Dog man : an uncommon life on a faraway mountain / Martha Sherrill.
        p. cm.
    ISBN 978-1-59420-124-0
    1. Akita dog—Japan. 2. Sawataishi, Morie. 3. Human-animal relationships—Japan. I. Title
SF429.A65S55 2008   2007035113
636.73—dc22
[B]

PRINTED IN THE UNITED STATES OF AMERICA

10 9 8 7 6 5 4 3 2 1

For Kitako

And in memory of Bernard L. Knapp,
who loved Japan too

CONTENTS

This rare old tree is what we came to see.

—GARY SNYDER, *No Nature*

Introduction

There are mountain villages and green valleys throughout Japan, and very few people live in them. The cities teem and buzz with life—each year with increasing speed and sophistication, more crowds and smaller cell phones and a dizzying parade of manmade pleasures. But far away, the snow country world moves quietly, almost forgotten except as a dream. This is the story of that dream. It's about one man's devotion to a place and way of being, however preposterous it may seem to others, and how he gently, and not so gently, steers his life there.

Dogs were part of the dream—and came along. Every morning and evening Morie (*Mor-ee-ay*) walked with them into the dark woods and snowy mountains. Together, they traveled into a deeper place, the world of instinct and survival, investigating the subtleties of mountain life as well as its thrills and dangers. In the mountains, they encountered growling beasts and dead carcasses, poisonous mushrooms, flying pheasants and lost hikers. They fought off bugs and snakes and bears, and always came home, always, even if they'd gotten very lost themselves. Morie and his dogs were heroes every morning, and heroes again every night. With each walk into the wild, they were bold and resourceful. They were alive and alert, their senses acute, poised for the natural excitements that the rest of us must crave when we turn to flickering screens for adventures and when we ache to connect with nature and animals. We yearn for the company of dogs because they return us to an ancient way of life, vanishing now. It is the power of the natural world to reacquaint us with our quieter selves, the part now buried alive in the noise and glare of modern life and the new habit of nonstop connection with others.

If Morie lived in Alabama, he would have gone into the swamps with a coonhound. If he lived in Russia or Norway, he'd have crossed the tundra with a Karelian bear dog or a laika. Since he spent most of his life in the snow country of Japan, he roamed the rice fields and mountains with a traditional snow country dog, an ancient dog type or breed that's gone by different names over the centuries but has been called the "Akita" since 1927. Canine geneticists suspect the dogs came to the main island of Japan with the first tribes of migratory hunters two thousand years ago. They survived as companions to Ainu hunters, or *matagi*, who traveled the primeval forests and volcanic ranges in search of large game like bear and deer. After centuries of migrating, as people settled into the towns and small ports in the north, the dogs settled with them—and became primarily fighting dogs. They competed in village dog rings and other more casual gambling venues. Feudal lords collected them as living trophies and for several hundred years, from the sixteenth to the nineteenth century, the warrior class, the samurai, were inspired by the dogs' courage and rugged fighting spirit. For a particular type of samurai infantryman in training, an Akita dog was his teacher.

It never really mattered what the dogs looked like. Their essence or spirit was the quality most sought after—and valued. A good dog was quiet and fearless, could approach a cornered bear and prompt it to chase, and was virtually weatherproof. In recent times there's been a rather heated debate about what an Akita should look like, but from centuries ago, and still today, they share certain traits: a tightly curled tail, erect or "prick" ears, long and heavy legs. They resemble in many ways the dogs from the North all over the globe—dogs from cold climates and snowy Arctic regions, working dogs that have been used for centuries to pull sleds or hunt big game. They have hearty appetites, eating as much as eight or nine pounds of food a day, great stamina, sharp hunting instincts, and a thick double coat of fur that's heavy enough to allow them to burrow deep in the snow and sleep there. During a blizzard, flakes of wet snow stick to their coat and cover it completely, insulation that keeps them even warmer.

From a certain perspective, they can seem out of sync with modern times. The Akita is a noble dog, graceful and quiet, as well as an ancient dog—recent genetic studies have shown it to be one of a handful of the most primitive breeds, linked closely to the wolf—but some of its traits can make it a little rough for polite company. Vestigial instincts lead it to confrontation and overprotection. Until just ninety years ago, the small towns and villages in the snow country competed against each other in the dog ring, which explains why Akitas today can display aggressiveness toward other dogs and small animals, usually less dominant ones. In its milder expression, an Akita's overprotectiveness can resemble devotion or emotional attachment. It can look like love. Unlike some of the other ancient breeds, an Akita forms an unusually strong bond with its owner. They are famously loyal to the human families or the packs to which they belong.

Loyalty is a trait of dogs in general—along with begging, lingering, wheedling, and persistence—but from a Western perspective, the Akita's sense of loyalty can be extreme and result in unwanted situations. Akita dogs are fiercely protective of family members, to the point of attacking benign intruders: the postman, the plumber, the unsuspecting Jehovah's Witness. They have been known to travel hundreds of miles and endure hardships in order to reunite with their owners, which can make it difficult to give an Akita away. There's also a tendency for strange, almost miraculous determination.

The sled dogs that inspired the story of the Disney movie *Eight Below*—the dogs that were left behind on a research base in Antarctica and survived alone while they waited for their master's return—were not huskies but Japanese Karafuto dogs, close cousins to the Akita. As the account goes, the two surviving dogs, named Taro and Jiro, ran to their scientist owner with wild enthusiasm and slobbering affection despite the fact that they'd been abandoned by him for an entire year in arctic conditions.

The most beloved dog in Japanese history, Hachi-ko, is an example of this same kind of forbearance and need to cling to pack rituals and remain loyal to the leader. After his owner—a well-known Tokyo University professor—suffered a stroke at work in 1924 and subsequently died, the Akita appeared at the Shibuya train station every afternoon for nine years and watched the commuters disembark from the four o'clock train, looking for the professor to appear. As the years passed, newspaper accounts were written about Hachi-ko, postcards of the aging dog and other souvenirs were sold at the train station, and a bronze sculpture was erected while the real dog was still alive to stand nearby. Tourists began gathering there (it is still a famous gathering spot in Tokyo), a Hachi-ko fan club was established, and soon afterward the ministry of education had a song written, *"Chu-ken Hachi-ko"* or "Loyal Hachi-ko," which was taught to schoolchildren nationwide as a lesson in the importance of loyalty, a bit of propaganda to benefit the emperor.

As far as anybody knows, the first Akita appeared on the shores of the United States about a decade later. Helen Keller had four collies at home already, but when she traveled to Japan in 1937 on a ten-week speaking tour of Asia, the internationally celebrated deaf and blind author was so moved by the story of Hachi-ko, she announced on the spot that she wanted a dog just like him. She was presented, almost immediately, with an Akita puppy. His name, Kamikaze-Go (translated as "divine wind"), didn't carry the same unfortunate association in 1937 that it would a few years later. In any case, Keller called him "Kami" and kept him in her first-class cabin during the long ocean voyage from Yokohama to San Francisco and in her private train car to the Mayo Clinic in Rochester and on to New York City, where newspaper reporters were waiting at the station to meet this new kind of dog from the exotic Far East.

"If there was ever an angel in fur, it was Kamikaze," she wrote to unburden herself when Kami died of distemper a few months later. "I know I shall never feel quite the same tenderness for any other pet." The dog had "all the qualities that appeal to me—he is gentle, companionable and trusty . . . an unfailing source of happiness. I never saw such devotion in a five month old puppy."

Arrangements were made for a littermate of Kamikaze's to be sent to Keller as an official gift of the Japanese government in 1938. In years to come, Keller would describe the special spiritual connection she felt with her second Akita, whom she called Go-Go. He had a strong soulful presence, she said, and quiet confidence. In interviews she remarked on how serene he was, how attentive and careful. The dog had figured out very quickly that she was blind, she said, and

Keller and Go-Go say hello

never got underfoot. He walked gracefully throughout her grand house in Westport, Connecticut, without disturbing the antiques. As Keller put it, "his every move suggests, 'I know who I am.'"

Morie Sawataishi wasn't drawn to the Akita because it was exotic. For him, it was simply the local dog, the regional dog, the breed he'd seen everywhere as a child growing up in the snow country. Common as a weed, they were the hometown breed, a country dog— almost, I'm afraid to say, the neglected and rather overlooked native variety. In those days in Japan, if you wanted to impress people, you had a German shepherd.

He was thirty years old before he owned his first dog. He just had a hunch, a gut instinct, that he should get one. Maybe the old story of Hachi-ko tugged at him, he says. But it was 1944 and the snow country dogs were being slaughtered for their pelts—the military paid dearly, and used them to line the officers' coats. By the time the war ended, a year later, there were only a dozen or so Akita dogs left in Japan. Two of them belonged to Morie.

THIS IS A BOOK that desires to be specific and personal rather than general and historical. It is not a book about Japan. And while it reveres culture and history as forces that can dwarf and bend our lives, it doesn't assume that we are blown like dead leaves by time and circumstances into predictable piles. It is not written in support of the Great Man theory either, in which the reader is supposed to be convinced, by the end of the book, that only a small minority of magnificently talented souls are able to make a dent in the monolith of recorded time. Morie Sawataishi does not aspire to dent. He is aware of the monolith and tries to exist peacefully beside it, but not so close that it casts too great a shadow on him.

Years ago, Morie had a dream about what he wanted his life to be like, what he hoped his days would add up to and come to mean. It wasn't a borrowed dream or a lifestyle collage he'd made from reading books or watching movies or looking at advertisements in a magazine. Morie came up with it on his own—and against all odds.

When he built his house in the mountains, his kingdom of the dogs was miles from nowhere. You walked down the steep driveway and came to a small country road that wound along the edge of a mountain lake and then gently descended into a valley of rice fields. It was quiet and still, and in the early morning, you heard only the sounds of nightingales. Nowadays things are a little different. The road at the bottom of Morie's driveway is wider and cars speed along the lake, restless as sharks, and quickly disappear inside a tunnel.

If you join the speeding cars and enter the tunnel, you will find yourself on a highway passing rice farmers on their tractors and small greenhouses and barns. Keep going to another valley dotted with convenience stores and a few billboards and, after forty minutes or so, you will wind up at a station for the bullet train. You can buy newspapers in the station, and food to go. There are televisions propped up on the walls, and suspended from ceilings, broadcasting colorful shows of every kind. Once aboard the cool white modern coach of the train, you'll soon pick up speed and be moving in a swift straight hush toward one of the largest cities on earth. The scenery of the snow country as you leave it becomes a blur. But when you think back to Morie's house with its one black dial telephone and tatami mats, its beautiful old teacups, handmade snowshoes, ancient dog show trophies, stuffed swan, and the empty wasp's nest that hangs like a treasure in his foyer, it will seem as though you have traveled, in less than an hour, through decades, even centuries. You have gone from then to now. You have left a slow and quiet world like your grandfather's, or great grandfather's, and have returned to modern life.

You might be happy coming back to your own place and time, but after you've been to the snow country and met Morie and his dogs, the modern world won't feel quite the same way again. That is why this book exists. It's a way to continue to be with Morie, and also to understand him and ourselves.

One

Opening the Mountain

The house is hard to see, low and camouflaged by foliage, encased in green, almost swallowed whole by nature. Across a dark glassy lake and halfway up a foothill of Mount Kurikoma, a red roof shimmers like an old sequin dropped long ago among the cedars. You could miss the narrow entrance if your car is going too quickly, if you're trying to get your cell phone to work, if your mind is taken up with familiar things.

Morie is especially proud of the location. He built the house thirty years ago against quite an array of obstacles. The most formidable was his family: His wife was against it, and his kids. Even his in-laws objected. Morie didn't let any of them get to him. The next layer of disapproval was social: Why wasn't he aspiring to an easy life of golf and warm sunshine like all the other successful men in Japan? Why did he want something so unusual? Next came financial obstacles, and bureaucratic—permits and paperwork—and finally, the sheer logistical nightmare of building a house so far from anything. Morie didn't let any of that stuff bother him too much either.

He made a few jokes and complained at dinner to a table of family members who were largely enjoying his problems, but otherwise Morie remained calm and persistent. He plugged along. He had a vision of what kind of life he wanted for himself—what kind of days, what kind of nights, even what kind of air. He knew what kind of mountain vegetables he liked (just picked), what kind of snowfalls (heavy), what kind of woods (shadowy), and even what kind of surprises he hoped to encounter around the bend of mountain trails (bears, wild antelope, maybe a lost and distraught hiker). He imagined his future, you might say. And the dogs led him to it.

It's spectacularly clear tonight. The wind is loud and whirring and low clouds are blowing off to other parts of the snow country. The sky is alive with glittering stars and a rising moon. Below them, the house is dark but for a faint blue light coming from the kitchen where Atsuko has left some breakfast for her parents: broth for soup, warm rice, two fresh mackerel to grill in a small gas oven.

The alarm goes off at 2:15 a.m. and Morie lingers in bed for a while, moves his legs around under the down blanket and rolls onto his side. He's a big guy with broad shoulders and a barrel chest, but he looks pretty sweet with his bald head resting on the small buckwheat pillow. His face is soft and pink. His skin is thin, and smooth as a child's. In the dim light of the room, his eyes are open.

He looks over at his wife in her twin bed across the room. He can see Kitako's gray hair and the outline of her high cheekbones. He can hear her breathing deeply.

Just another minute. Then he'll get up. Just one more. It takes discipline—and a certain concentration of energy—to get up at two in the morning, no matter what age you are. Morie isn't young. He can't even call himself middle-aged. But thinking about being beaten to the top of the mountain suddenly propels him out of bed. One swift motion and he's on his feet. It seems a well-practiced move, like one of his judo exercises.

It's funny which habits stay with us, unconsciously, and which traditions continue, however old we get. Morie isn't one of those people who's compulsive about routine or observing all the ceremonies of his country, or honoring every single old way of doing something simply because it's traditional or Shinto—the native folk religion in Japan. But he does quite joyfully participate in the tradition of *O-Yama-biraki*, Open Mountain Day. Each year in the third week of May, people in this corner of Japan celebrate the passage of time and the warming of the days by walking to the top of the mountain. What began as a Shinto ritual has endured as an annual hiking holiday with a spiritual component—without making a pretentious fuss of it, you are respecting the mysteries of the wild, the endurance of the mountain, the fleeting seasons, things so profoundly understood in the snow country that they are hardly worth discussing.

The thinking goes like this: Mount Kurikoma is a spirit that's been slumbering, covered by snow since December. As the days grow warmer, the mountain slowly awakens. In March, the lake begins to swell with the mountain's melted water. In April, the sunshine is stronger and the valley floods. Rice seedlings are planted. The plum trees blossom with delicate clouds of white petals. A week or two later, the cherry trees burst into clusters of pink bloom that don't wither as much as jump from their branches and land on earth like confetti. Not long after, the slopes below Morie's house explode in azalea and rhododendron blooms so profuse and showy, so multicolored and outrageous, it's almost hard to believe. Even this morning, in the luminous moonlight, Morie's slope looks like the grand finale of a fireworks show.

Mount Kurikoma has a small cap of snow, but by the third week of May, the trails to its summit are finally passable and the danger of avalanche is over. The long snow country winter has passed—and the mountain comes alive again. Morie shakes alive again too. Each year on Open Mountain Day, he and Kitako rise hours before dawn and hike up the slushy paths with the dogs. It's still dark when they reach the top.

When it comes to opening the mountain, Morie likes to be first.

It's a matter of pride, really. He's an ancient relic, he knows, but even so, Morie has a reputation he likes to protect. He's still Morie Sawataishi no matter how old he manages to get. When the full heat of summer comes in August, he'll turn eighty-nine, but being joyfully competitive is part of his nature—and a kind of personal tradition that has stayed with him. It's his way of keeping up appearances. Each year, a couple of weeks after his spectacular dogs and their descendants are triumphant at the big show in Odate, Morie likes to open the mountain before anybody else. But each year, it gets a little harder. Hiking has become popular in Japan, along with the romance of the outdoors and a craving for something a popular magazine has branded "The Slow Life." Even city people arrive at dawn to climb Mount Kurikoma these days, so Morie has to get up a little earlier to beat them. For years, getting up at 3:30 was enough. Then it was 3:00. Last year, in 2003, he and Kitako set the alarm for 2:30. Now it's 2:15.

Unspeakably early. Painfully early. The idiotic bantam rooster is still asleep and all the dogs are out cold. Morie has three Akitas now. The younger ones, Little Guy and Fox, are pale golden dogs with auburn tinges and a white mask. Their kennels are behind the house, near the chicken coop and across from the shed where Morie dries persimmons on strands of ropes and shiitake mushrooms on slated wooden shelves. Shiro, the pack leader, lives out front on the crest of the driveway in a large kennel with a red roof and red bars like an old circus cage. Except to use the word *cage* or *kennel*, or even *doghouse*, doesn't do justice to where Morie's dogs live. Trained as an engineer, and reflexively resourceful, Morie designed all the kennels to receive just the right amount of sunlight, the right amount of cool shade. Each of them has separate areas, or rooms, for sleeping, eating, and defecating. They are open to the sky and also, in parts, covered by a metal roof that's angled so the heavy northern snow will slide off and land in a place that Morie won't have to dig around.

Shiro lifts his head. It's almost as if he knows he's being talked about. Akitas are famous for their keenness, and spooky sixth sense, but if you don't buy that explanation, it's possible that Shiro lifts his head because he hears Morie shuffling around inside the house or because he smells a pot of green tea steeping in the dining room. Shiro's the sentinel dog, in any case. From his spot at the top of the driveway, he greets all and sees all: the lake, the mountain, the house, the azalea fireworks display in the garden. He's a creamy-white dog, the biggest Akita that Morie has raised in a long time, and a national champion many times over. There's a hall of fame for Akitas in Japan, and Shiro's in it. Even an untrained eye can see that there's something superb about him. At thirteen and verging on what should be decrepit, the dog continues to be handsome and vigorous. His coat is so thick the fur looks like it is permanently standing on end.

He rises suddenly. His tail is wagging, almost like a pom-pom in a cheerleader's hand. He lifts his head and lets out a long slow lonely howl. It's not defensive or threatening, like a growl or bark. It's a declaration. More powerful than any computer-enhanced cry from a Harry Potter movie, the sound is unearthly, eerie—no, beyond that. It's a lamentation that awakens a forgotten energy

Shiro at thirteen

inside you, something true and essential and wild that seems buried beneath years of civilization.

Could Shiro know what morning it is? Maybe the length of the days or the warmth of the ground has told him it's time to open the mountain. Maybe a certain smell has told him, or a combination of smells that come together every year at this time. Each week in the snow country is a revelation of new sounds, too. The spring peepers in the rice paddies have started their calls at dusk. As sunrise approaches, the nightingales sing their haunting loopy songs.

What else tells Shiro that it is Open Mountain Day? For the last two weeks, Morie has been snapping off the small curling tops of the fiddlehead ferns when he takes the dogs for a run down by the dam and Shiro likes to smell the broken stems. He likes to drink the newly melted mountain water too. He can drink and drink and drink.

Morie slides open the door to the garden. He's wearing a pair of inky jeans and a puffy green parka, a pair of silver high-tech hiking sneakers that look like space shoes. His bald head is covered in a white kerchief, old style, like a worn-out warrior in an Akira Kurosawa movie.

Shiro jumps on the sides of his kennel. He's more excited than usual this morning, almost frenzied. (Maybe he can smell the can of spray paint in Morie's pocket?) He's fixated on Morie's every move. All of Morie's dogs are utterly fascinated with him—and excited by his movements. They are observers of Morie, devotees of Morie. Whatever Morie does, they want to know about it, and seem to be making a constant assessment of whether they should be involved or not.

On the other side of the house, Little Guy and Fox start barking. Younger than Shiro and more excitable, they are jumping up again and again on the fencing.

When Morie opens the door to their kennels, they jump on him too. He never trained them not to jump. He never trained them to "sit" and "stay" or "shake" either. Those commands seem ridiculous and humiliating to him. Mountain dogs don't need to shake anybody's hand. He dislikes any humanizing. You might as well dress them up in T-shirts and sunglasses, the way the young girls in Tokyo costume their Chihuahuas and dachshunds for the subway.

Besides, Morie says jumping is good for a dog's spine. And it's a natural thing, the way dogs are. Why would you want to stop dogs from being dogs?

The shape and appearance of his Akitas have changed dramatically in the last six decades since Morie has been raising them. Their bodies are leaner and their coats fit more snugly on their bodies. Their tails are more perfectly curled. Little Guy and Fox and Shiro have a narrower head and a more delicate snout than Morie's dogs from the 1950s and '60s—more like a fox's head than a shepherd's—and their eyes are triangular, more almond-shaped than round. In the old days of Japan, honoring the idea of a specific look or "breed" was never part of the dog tradition. Spirit was the thing one hoped to keep alive. Nowadays Morie complains that the dogs have gone in the wrong direction. While they might be prettier, they've gotten weaker over the years; their primitive instincts are fading, and their ruggedness. But still there's something special about their nature that's evident in their expression.

Akitas have an unusual look on their faces, a gaze that seems penetrating and vigilant. Unlike most dogs, Little Guy and Fox and Shiro don't seem to be waiting for guidance, or food, or affection; they seem to be making keen note of the world and waiting for the next big thing to happen. It's a calm look, detached—almost cold. Perhaps it is the look of a wolf. And to Morie, this quality is as essential to a

Jumping is good for the spine

good snow country dog as the double coat of fur. An Akita doesn't have to be aesthetically beautiful or even conform perfectly to all sixty-seven standards of the breed, but it should be alert and ready for anything.

A door slides open. Morie looks up. The dogs look up too. Kitako is putting on her boots. She's wearing a fleece hat over her chin-length hair and a paisley wool scarf around the shoulders of her powdery blue coat. She's moving quickly, full of energy. She seems as excited to open the mountain as the dogs. Morie gives her a puzzled look, as if to say, "What's up with you?"

"Good morning," Kitako says to him with a nod. She always says "good morning" to him in an upbeat voice. She always bows with a quick nod, and offers a smile. Morie takes all this morning behavior for granted—her nod, her smile, the way she greets him cheerfully every single day as if she really means it. But this morning Kitako seems almost exuberant.

Maybe she's thinking this is the last time they'll open the mountain together. She keeps talking about how old they are, and how they might have to quit hiking. She seems focused on this—and a bit sharp. Morie just ignores it. He never wants to engage on this topic. His feeling: Maybe so. Who knows? Why talk about it?

Buddhism teaches that life doesn't deliver completely black and white experiences, people only make them that way in their heads. But Kitako used to be pretty black and white on the subject of life in the snow country. She detested the mountains when they first married. She was raised in Azabu, an elegant neighborhood of Tokyo where the millionaires live. She wasn't a country girl. She was an *Azabu Gyaru*, or Azabu Girl—and quite modern and sophisticated when Morie married her in 1940. She wore high heels, stockings, and Western-style suits and had a teaching degree. She'd never been to the snow country. She'd never been outside Tokyo. Morie knew her brother at Yokosuka Naval Academy and stayed with the Kato family while he looked for a job after finishing his service with the military in 1939. The Katos were a bit fancy, and refined, and educated—they knew famous writers and poets, and one of Kitako's sisters spoke English—but Morie had managed to impress them, even though he was from the north and had a thick country accent and booming voice. His manners weren't perfect either. But he was handsome, with a full head of hair in those days, and taller than the other guys, and stronger. He might have been smarter, too. The best and brightest men of his generation were in the navy. He never said a word about wanting to move back to the snow country and live in the sticks. Not a word. And who would suspect that anybody who'd gotten out of the north would ever want to return? A star at the academy and a decorated hero of the Sino-Japanese War, Morie was swamped with job offers from big engineering companies in Tokyo. Kitako's parents were glad to see their daughter wind up with such a clever man who'd keep her nearby—and approved of the marriage without apparent reservations. Kitako didn't seem to have any reservations either. But after their wedding in Tokyo, when Morie brought his young wife home to meet his family in Akita prefecture, Kitako's first impressions of the snow country weren't very positive.

After meeting Morie's family and having a long afternoon meal at their house, Kitako had said to Morie: "Where do we go tonight?" In Tokyo, they'd gone out every night—bars, nightclubs, coffee shops—and it hadn't occurred to her that their marriage would be any different, or that they might find themselves anywhere but the exclusive neighborhood where she'd been raised. Arriving in Gojome-machi, or Castle No. 5 Town, the small village where Morie grew up, she hadn't even looked around long enough to see that there wasn't a nightclub or coffeehouse or even a restaurant. "Where do we go tonight?" she had asked her new husband. There were glorious mountains and lakes, forests and rivers and hot springs. On a clear day, you could see the sparkling blue water of the Sea of Japan in the distance. But no nightlife.

How did she wind up here? From the very first day of her marriage, that had been the main refrain of her life, hadn't it? Or maybe she'd been too sheltered to imagine a place like the snow country could exist, that an entire region of Japan could be so slow and quiet, where people gravitated outdoors in the morning, to toil in the fields or gather mushrooms on the mountain, and fall into bed early at night. No bars. No clubs. Nothing but a black sky of stars and the sound of the wind. Now, at the age of eighty-three, here she is, bounding out of the house in the middle of the night, well before dawn, to hike up the mountain in the slush. She can't even hide her enthusiasm. Morie seems not to notice, in any case. He was mostly indifferent to her complaints over the years and tries to be indifferent to her enthusiasms now. She's moving so quickly, though. She must think it's the last time they'll open the mountain together.

Morie doesn't like to consider the possibility. He doesn't dwell on the road ahead too much, and he doesn't want to spend time contemplating the far future, or even the near future that's completely unknowable anyhow. You don't have to dwell and worry to be prepared for everything. When you worry, or start looking too closely at the road ahead, it can upset your equilibrium. Morie likes to exist in the present with enthusiasm, wariness, a mix of readiness and calm. He doesn't need worries to make him vigilant. He and the dogs have the same approach: They suspect that a good meal or a walk or a drink of cold mountain water is just around the corner—or maybe a black bear with a white crescent blaze on its chest. The mountain isn't as dangerous as it once was. But the bears are still there.

Dwelling in the past is another thing. Morie and Kitako kept scrapbooks and photo albums for years and never looked at them. Looking back seemed like a waste of time—a luxury. But since their oldest daughter Atsuko and her husband came to live at the house, Morie's been luxuriating more, and reflecting. Upstairs he had squirreled away boxes and boxes of dog trophies, medals, ribbons, certificates, pedigrees, show catalogs, old collars and leashes. It took Atsuko three months to organize all the dog stuff and bring it downstairs into the tatami room and stash it in the deep Japanese closets. They made jokes about all the trophies. Why are the new trophies so huge? Impossible to store! Now you slide open the closet doors in the tatami room and all you see are trophies stacked on top of each other, lying sideways, jumbled up, like you've come upon a glorious golden treasure—except of course it's mostly cheap metal and gold paint. The trophies are like that now, kind of cheesy and worthless and too big.

Sometimes Morie comes across a photograph of one dog and leaves it on the dining table. One picture. A day's worth of thought. A week's worth. He enjoys memories, almost like food. He took the photographs himself with a camera that he couldn't afford, but bought anyway in 1944, and he developed the film in a large closet of their first house in Hachimantai. He remembers standing in his makeshift darkroom and watching the images appear on the white paper, like magic, the pictures of dogs swirling in photographic fluid.

THE PAST SEEMS like a landscape of choices—things rejected, things embraced—decisions that take you down new paths that twist and ascend, or descend, and suddenly you are walking in a new place. Your life has been changed, but sometimes it happens so slowly that you don't know it, until you look back. Yesterday he spent the afternoon digging inside a box of loose pictures. He got to laughing, and then Kitako appeared and laughed beside him.

Each dog picture brings back a feeling, a whole atmosphere—a different smell, a different view of life, different expectations. Each generation of dogs was distinct. Morie remembers the color and thickness of their fur, how solid their bodies were, how their tails curled, or didn't, and whether their ears were erect. He remembers which dogs were good hunters, which were good mothers, and he knows their names—much better than the names of the people who occasionally appear in his photographs. A sister-in-law? Which one? There were so many—it's a fog of in-laws. But his memory of each dog seems pristine.

There have been a hundred dogs, literally. An unimaginable number. "It doesn't matter how many dogs you have," he says. "When you lose one, it always feels terrible."

He can't remember the name of the first dog he owned. He was thirty. Kitako was pregnant with their second child. Morie remembers buying the dog, and bringing it home. He remembers Kitako's reaction. (How angry she was.) Morie remembers all that clearly. But the name? "It wasn't a time for names," he says finally. "We just called her dog."

The rest had names. After No Name, there was Three Good Lucks—what a sweet, smart, beautiful red dog. Just thinking about him makes Morie emit a charming singsong growl, like he's savoring every memory of that time. He's got lots of pictures of One Hundred Tigers—so promising, really, until he lost his tail in the fence. Victory Princess was another spectacular white dog. She was a beauty with a difficult temperament, a bit of a biting problem. When she had puppies, she wouldn't let Morie come near them. She snapped if he tried. "Some mothers are like that," Morie says, "and you have to respect them." Victory Princess had lots of great puppies too.

It goes on and on. Hoko. Homan. Happiness. There aren't too many pictures of Samurai Tiger, but it turns out that Morie was so crazy about him, and so busy training him, hunting with him, and winning titles with him, that he didn't bother with the camera much. So if you want to talk about Samurai Tiger it might take awhile. He was a dog you can't just mention in passing one afternoon, between cups of tea. Samurai Tiger deserves a whole night and lots of sake. And it will take a few hours to get to the awful part.

Morie chokes up sometimes when he thinks about it, or studies a picture of Samurai Tiger. The dog's courage and spirit and energy are obvious, even in snapshots, and when Morie's mind dwells on it, his face scrunches so you can't see his eyes anymore and his mouth shuts tight. He starts to cry—just a little—and his voice becomes higher under the strain of trying not to. "Oh," he growls, "I've lived too long!"

BY THE TIME Morie and Kitako arrive at the first mountain pass, the sky is turning orange below the horizon of the green valley. It's still dark, so they use a flashlight to see the trail. They don't talk much. They watch the dogs vanishing behind mounds of snow. After about five kilometers, the rough equivalent of three miles, they reach the end of an access road where the snowplows stopped and left a tall bank of snow—it's really a wall of snow, twenty or thirty feet high.

Morie reaches into his coat pocket for the can of spray paint. The cap is red. He shakes it, and the small metal balls ping and tumble against the can. The dogs jump at the sound and gather around Morie. He raises his arm and sprays two red characters on the snow wall, each of them about three feet high:

万 歳

They spell out *banzai*. It's an out-of-date expression in Japan, the kind of thing an old goat like Morie would say. Literally it means "ten thousand years," but foreigners usually associate it with World War II, when Japanese soldiers were supposed to cry out, *Tennouheika Banzai!* or "Long Live the Emperor!" just before they died. Really, it's just a general exclamation of enthusiasm, and triumph, which can be congratulatory or self-congratulatory, depending on the setting and subject. If you do something good, or you're proud of yourself, you might say, *Banzai! Banzai! Banzai!* You'd do this in a crowd of people, or when you've won the lottery or a game of tennis. It's akin to cheering *hurray!* or pumping your fist while using that popular nineties expression, *Yesssssss!*

Morie's hand rises with the spray can again. He adds three more characters:

秋 田 犬

Dogs. Specifically, Akita dogs. The wall of snow will be there for a week or two before melting and he likes to imagine all the hikers who'll come along and see that, once again, crazy Morie was there first.

Banzai Akita!

Hurray, you beautiful dogs. Hurray!

Two

No Name

Her fur was brown and black and gray, flecked with small dashes of color. Her ears and mask were black, as well as the beauty mark on her left cheek. Her eyes were dark and watchful. She was quiet, rarely barked, as if she knew that she was being hidden. It was remarkable how catlike a dog could be.

No Name was a small fork in a trail that became a path, then a road, then a highway that took Morie to a place he never returned from.

THE FEELING CAME ON SUDDENLY. It was inexplicable, almost mystical. Morie had never owned a dog before or thought of owning one. As a boy in Castle No. 5 Town, he spent hours wandering the green hills and fishing in the mountain streams, but never dreamed about having a dog with him. He played along the shore of the vast lake, the second largest on the main island of Japan, and never once thought about having a dog along, or tossing a stick to him in the water. Morie's father was a big shot in town, a local politician and businessman who had kennels of fighting dogs, and Morie had never liked them. The dogs were aggressive and scary and barked incessantly. Morie and his brothers and sisters weren't allowed to approach them, let alone play with them. In Akita prefecture, there were all kinds of rich important men who kept dogs for the ring in those days—a sure way to impress everybody—and they hired dog boys to tend to the dirty work, the feeding and training, the breeding and exercising. Morie had never wanted to be a dog boy, or a dog man, for that matter. The prospect couldn't have been less appealing.

Then one day in 1944 when he was thirty years old, Morie wanted a dog. It came on like a sudden urge or craving. He tried to resist it— what kind of fool kept a dog when the government had made it almost impossible to have one? But he'd start wanting a dog all over again.

It was wartime and everything was difficult. But then, for Morie, it had always been wartime and everything had always been difficult. Since he was a kid, Japan had been on a rampage—invading other countries, pillaging, enslaving, overtaking . . . always, they were told, for the good of Japan, for the good of the world, spreading the emperor's truth to the globe. Morie's father had served in Japan's war with Russia, and Morie's older brothers had fought in China. When Morie graduated from the academy in 1933, the Imperial Navy sent him to several fronts in Manchuria and China, where he'd fought and killed in battles and seen hundreds of his countrymen die, and cheated death himself—more than once. In 1939 when he was discharged, he was happy to be free and hoped the warring might be over. Instead, it escalated. Eighteen months after Morie got out of the navy, Japan declared war on the United States and its allies, and by the time he started to crave his first dog, millions of

Japanese had died in combat, and millions were starving at home. Air strikes on the cities of Japan kept coming, and coming, city blocks turning to rubble and ash, city after city. Nobody could remember when things had been bleaker.

Morie and Kitako were living in Hachimantai then, a remote and beautiful corner of the snow country, far away from the air raids and fires. Morie had been sent there by Mitsubishi, a large engineering conglomerate in Tokyo. The position came with a house, an old-style wooden Japanese residence, quite large and grand, a former summer house of an aristocratic family and now owned by Morie's company. Getting to the plant took only a few minutes on foot but getting anywhere else was an ordeal. Morie drove a horse cart into the village for provisions and Kitako sometimes walked the five miles with a toddler hanging on her back. Things were easier in the summer when vegetables and fruit grew in the garden and there were fish to catch in the streams behind the house, but in winter food was harder to come by. The north had always struggled with poverty and severe weather, but now things were dire. The rice crop disappeared to feed soldiers, and other supplies were rationed or simply impossible to obtain.

Morie had a good job in the snow country while the war with the United States kept going on and on. He was employed by Mitsubishi to supervise the construction and operation of a growing string of new hydroelectric plants. He was a little like Midas, except rather than gold, he brought light and energy and warmth with him wherever he roamed. The prefecture of Akita was famous for its pure water, wonderful rice, delicious sake, strong dogs, and pale, beautiful women. But the land was rugged and largely undeveloped, and there was no electricity outside the larger cities of Odate and Akita, and few telephones or cars. While Tokyo glittered with street lights and neon, and its residents kept warm with gas heaters, in the snow country the oil lamp and lantern were the only sources of evening light—besides the moon. Even candles were rare.

A handful of dams had been built already, and now hydroelectric plants were coming. Morie was the god of electricity, greasing the wheels, laying the groundwork, and meeting with local village leaders all over the north. He was good at this, awfully good. He loved to sit and drink, to talk about country things. And the deal was simple: if a village made room for a dam and a power plant, often requiring some farms and farmers to be relocated, all the villagers would get electricity for life—for free. The response was always unanimous: There wasn't a place in the north that didn't welcome a plant, or a snow country house that didn't slide open its doors and offer Morie Sawataishi some food or a cup of sake.

Sometimes he'd go off on a pair of cross country skis to visit a prospective village, get snowed in, and be gone for a week. On one such trip to a snow country town near Akita City, Morie had heard something so troubling that he couldn't put it out of his mind. It stuck there, like a worm. A doctor confided to him that country people were killing their dogs—and selling the pelts to the military. People were starving, and sometimes the dogs were being eaten, too. In any case, the government information agency had declared that it wasn't right to keep dogs as pets when there was so little food available. It was unpatriotic and selfish. If you had extra food you should be sharing it with your neighbors. If you had a good dog, it should be handed over. Otherwise the village police were ordered to take them. The military used some dogs for wartime purposes, usually to carry supplies, or they were loaded up with explosives and sent into enemy camps. They worked in the battlefields alongside soldiers—and courageous dog stories were always in the newspapers. But the military only wanted German shepherds for these missions. The Akitas were skinned and their fur was used to line the officers' winter coats, or to make fur vests. It was a deeply held custom in Japan—and a virtue—to use everything, every part of an animal, and not waste. But now it was becoming difficult to say how many Akitas were left.

The news twisted inside Morie. As he walked home in the deep snow, mile after mile, he couldn't stop thinking about what he'd heard. He didn't want to believe that people would really eat their dogs, but at the same time, he had an uncomfortable feeling it was probably true. And it was also probably true that the breed was almost extinct. Even before the war Akitas had been dwindling in number. They'd gone out of favor. And the ones remaining had been bred with foreign dogs—mastiffs, Great Danes, German shepherds, sometimes even a Saint Bernard. Foreign dogs were strong and huge and impressed everybody so much it was as if the Japanese forgot what an incredible dog they had already. People wanted new types of dogs, modern dogs, not some relic of the samurai days. Worried that the breed would disappear entirely, in 1927 a preservation society had been founded to save the Akita, and the government had declared the dog a protected species or "natural treasure" of Japan, but even that hadn't made them popular. Nothing seemed to.

Hachi-ko—the Akita who waited every afternoon at the Shibuya train station in Tokyo for his dead master to return—had partly been the inspiration behind the formation of the preservation society. Newspaper accounts had made the dog famous all over Japan and in 1935, the government had erected a statue of Hachi-ko on the spot where the dog waited. And while there were songs written about Hachi-ko, and souvenirs sold at the train station, and the preservation society had been established, the breed still wasn't very popular. To most people, they seemed like throwback dogs, hayseed dogs. After centuries of being bred for fighting and hunting, they could be rough and aggressive. And all those foreign dogs seemed more docile—and exotic.

Morie heard about an Akita puppy in a village just south of Odate. He'd run into a man named Tadao Yamazaki, a former taxi driver in Tokyo, who had a puppy that was very quietly for sale. It was almost illicit—like something you'd hear whispered about on the black market. Yamazaki told Morie that the puppy was a beautiful female, the descendant of a famous Akita named Chiharu, a dog that would eventually grace a postage stamp in 1953. Everybody knew what a spectacular dog Chiharu was, and Morie imagined that his granddaughter must be a fine dog too. But it was madness to think of bringing home a dog. In some snow country villages, the police were rounding dogs up and killing them. What would Kitako say? Again and again, Morie tried to put the puppy out of his head, but found that he couldn't.

He'd always been vaguely embarrassed by the government propaganda surrounding Hachi-ko—the way schoolchildren were taught the story as a lesson in devotion to the emperor. But it had really bothered Morie when he heard on the radio that the bronze statue of the dog had been melted down for metal. Who cares about a statue, right? Morie found himself thinking about it at odd times. It seemed like such an act of desperation. Maybe the story of Hachi-ko was exaggerated, and maybe the dog wasn't at the train station every single afternoon for nine years. Or maybe there were hundreds of other dogs who would've done the same thing. But propaganda aside, hype aside, Morie thought about the value of that kind of loyalty and faithfulness, and the preciousness of it—even the idea that loyalty of that kind could exist on earth. Whether the emperor's war was right or not: Who would be loyal as a dog if there weren't any dogs left?

He drove his horse cart over the dirt roads to Odate, a day's ride away at the cold end of winter. The puppy was as incredible as he'd heard—alert and trusting, a thick coat of fur, dark and soulful eyes. There wasn't one cell in Morie's body that could resist her, and even his bargaining for a better price was halfhearted. He got Yamazaki down from five hundred to three hundred yen, but still it was an outrageous amount of money. Three hundred yen. At the time, his salary was fifty yen a month.

All the way home, with the puppy in a box with a blanket, Morie wondered if he was a fool. But at the same time, he was happier than he'd felt in the longest time.

But what would he say to Kitako? He wasn't the sort of man to hide things from his wife—and hiding a puppy was impossible anyway. Morie had a woodshed behind the house and he cleared an area inside, made a bed for the puppy. Then he made a simple announcement to Kitako. He had a secret, he told her—something only she could know.

Kitako's initial thought: With so little food for anybody to eat, how can I feed a dog?

Then: What will the neighbors say?

Then she thought: *What kind of madman have I married?*

"I didn't talk to him for many days," Kitako says. "Maybe a week. Maybe longer."

They just called her "dog." Nothing cute, no nicknames either. She was peaceful, rarely barked, as if she knew she shouldn't. She grew to be stocky and strong. Her coat was salt and pepper—called *kurogoma*, or black sesame—and very thick. Her snout was long, like a shepherd's, and her tail wasn't so much curly as undecided.

Morie walked the puppy before dawn and again in the evening when the woods were dark and the neighbors wouldn't see him. He fed her quietly, by himself. After a few months, when the puppy started to look thin, Kitako began slipping her kitchen scraps during the day and confessed to Morie that she was worried. Was the puppy okay? Did it have worms? Kitako stopped complaining when Morie allowed her to put some rice into the dog's bowl.

During his days at the power plant, as the war with the United States dragged on and things grew steadily worse, and still worse again, after a burglar broke into their house and stole all their bedding, after the United States bombed the air base in Aomori, not too far away, and after Tokyo was firebombed and all his fancy in-laws started to arrive at his house needing food and shelter and safety, Morie would think about the beautiful dog in the shed at home and how magnificent it was. What a precious thing to have and to keep alive. What an honor it was, really. He began to design a bigger and better house for the dog, eventually using spare electric poles from the power plant. The new house looked like a log cabin. There was an indoor area in the front, and in the back, an open-air yard where the no-name granddaughter of Chiharu could sit in the sun, all alone, and nobody could see her.

KITAKO ISN'T SURE how long she went without speaking to her husband after the dog arrived. In those early days of their marriage, Kitako didn't yell. She just went mute, and tried to ignore him— even though she watched Morie carefully, and followed his every move. The house had a different feeling when they weren't speaking, as if the air had grown cold, as if all the rooms were empty or dead. She spent more time reflecting.

She couldn't remember, exactly, what was running through her head when she agreed to marry him. She was just twenty. "If the war weren't going on, I suspect I might have been more careful," she says. It was a confusing time, and confusing to think about. He made

a good impression, so tall and confident, and had things to offer—
strength and practical know-how, even pigheadedness—that could
get a wife and family through the worst of times. He gave off a sense
of security, even inimitability, the sort of permanence that you ache
for when your life seems up for grabs. Kitako might have been distracted by those qualities, she says, and not able to see how different
she and Morie were, or how differently they might want to live their
lives. His confidence and independent spirit were overshadowing,
and also, she says, beneath the roughness and booming voice, there
was something gentle about him, a sweetness in his eyes.

Their wedding took place in the spring of 1940. Morie wore a
black cutaway and tails. Kitako wore an exquisite ceremonial kimono
that had been her grandmother's. They had a Shinto service at the
Nogi Shrine in Tokyo, the site of the elegant residence where, nearly
thirty years before, General Maresuke Nogi and his wife Shizuko had
committed ritual suicide together. General and Mrs. Nogi were held
as paragons of virtue for killing themselves on the evening of
Emperor Meiji's funeral. In Japan it's called *junshi,* or "following
your lord in death," but that wasn't why Kitako chose the location. At
the time, the Nogi Shrine was simply the fanciest place for a high-
society girl to get married.

Instead of a proper honeymoon, the couple traveled north by
train to Castle No. 5 Town, a twenty-two-hour train ride in those
days, through rice fields and flat plains of open land and tunnels dug
in the steep mountains. At the end of this journey into the colder climate of the north, Morie's big family awaited them, his four older
brothers and five younger sisters, as well as his parents and an assortment of aunts and uncles. The house buzzed with excitement before
the young couple's arrival, while everybody cooked or cleaned or
made other preparations to celebrate.

Morie and Kitako on their wedding day, 1940

At the entrance to the house, where custom required that Morie and Kitako be formally greeted, the large and boisterous Sawataishi clan was stunned by the sight of a restrained young woman in a cutting-edge Western suit and high heels. Could this really be Morie's wife? She didn't even seem Japanese.

"I was a tomboy," says Haru, the youngest of the Sawataishi sisters, "and I'd never seen anybody wearing clothes like that before. A woman in a Western suit? It was almost unthinkable. Kitako-san was so sophisticated, and a beautiful speaker with an elegant voice—no Akita accent. *And she was from Tokyo.* Honestly, she might as well have been a foreigner or someone from another galaxy."

The younger sisters clamored around Kitako and reached out to feel the fabric of her suit. "Stand back! Get away!" Morie's mother shooed them away. "Give the girl some room. She's from a different kind of place than here. No touching! That's rude!"

Later that night, as welcoming as Morie's family had been, Kitako couldn't help feeling out of place in what seemed an isolated wilderness. "Where do we go tonight?" she'd asked Morie, who looked at her with an expression she didn't understand. It was so cold—still winter, with snow everywhere, as though spring was hesitant to arrive in such a serious place. And so dark—no streetlights or city lights, nothing but black sky and looming black mountains. She'd never been so far from the city, so far from anything remotely familiar. She grew even more lonesome the next morning when Morie announced that he'd decided to turn down a job offer in Tokyo. Instead, he had accepted a position with a Japanese company in Manchuria, not far from a recent war zone.

A breach opened between them. In those days, a man didn't have to consult his wife when career decisions were made, but on the other hand, consulting Kitako wouldn't have been a violation of Morie's manhood either, just a more refined and sophisticated approach, the kind of thing that would have been done routinely in Tokyo, but perhaps not the north. When Kitako returned home and told her family the news of Manchuria, her parents were vehemently against it, encouraging her to stand up to Morie and refuse to go. When she didn't feel comfortable making a stand on behalf of herself, Kitako's parents talked to their new son-in-law themselves. Manchuria was too far away, they said, and too dangerous. And their daughter was only twenty. Morie ignored their complaints, and even worse, ignoring their complaints seemed effortless for him. Manchuria was a colony of Japan and safe now, he calmly explained. In fact the government was encouraging Japanese to settle there. Working in Tokyo, like all the other men his age, didn't interest him, he said. Heading off to Manchuria was "an adventure," he told Kitako. "And you'll have an adventure too."

Kitako's memory of living in Manchuria in 1940 and 1941 is still vivid, "maybe because I was young and feeling very urgent about life—about wanting to see things and do things." What did she think of married life? She hadn't counted on having so little to do. Her teaching degree was useless in Manchuria and Morie worked constantly, first in a power plant, then for a submarine builder, then in a factory that made warplanes. And unlike in Tokyo, where she was surrounded by friends and family, Kitako made very few friends in her new home. Their first child was born on October 29 of the following year. Atsuko was moon-faced and looked like Morie. She was hearty and had a sense of humor. A baby was a new experience, but largely Kitako's experience.

She had help in the house—a Korean laundress, a Chinese housecleaner—and that was supposed to be the appealing thing about living in Manchuria. You could afford to have help. But eventually this became one of the aspects of living abroad that bothered Kitako most. The Japanese expansion into Manchuria had been particularly violent and the Manchurians, beleaguered and beaten down, carried a strong, lingering resentment of their conquerors, who were now immigrating in great numbers into their towns and cities. Kitako was shocked by the way her countrymen behaved in Manchuria, treating the Chinese like lesser beings, "as if they weren't really human," she says. And when she went to the market, she felt self-conscious, suspecting that she was hated by the local vendors simply for being Japanese, and for having money, and for maintaining a superior attitude that they assumed she had—and if she did, she was trying very quickly to erase it.

When she confided her feelings to Morie, she was relieved to hear he felt very much the same way. At the power plant, the Japanese bosses would kick or punch their Chinese workers—not a beating, exactly, but a humiliation, a daily abuse that made Morie sick to witness. He and Kitako had both seen their fellow Japanese demonstrate such insensitivity and cruelty, as well as this odd thing, a sense of being better than other people. In the small snow country town where Morie grew up, nobody acted that way. And Kitako? "I don't know where my feelings came from except that my grandmother used to take me to a Methodist church every Sunday when I was a girl," she says. "I didn't like going to church too much but I think certain things were ingrained in me. The minister spoke about the importance of treating all people the same, exactly as you'd want to be treated. This stayed with me. And in Manchuria, I suspected that other Japanese hadn't been exposed to this kind of thinking. That was the only excuse I could think of."

As a form of protest, Morie and Kitako made friends with some of the Chinese engineers at Morie's plant and invited them to the house for drinks and dinner. "Our Japanese colleagues and acquaintances were shocked and disapproved," Kitako says. "We didn't pay any attention to them."

When war broke out with the United States in December 1941, all Japanese civilians who were living outside the country were ordered back to Japan. Morie was away on a submarine when the announcement came, so Kitako returned alone with two-month-old Atsuko. They took a four-day train to the coast of Manchuria, then a steamer to Kyushu, then another train to Tokyo. Kitako packed only what she could carry, a small suitcase, and "left the rest behind or gave it away to people we knew." She brought only two diapers, she remembers, and when one became dirty, she washed it by hand in the small train bathroom sink and then held it out the window to dry.

The train cars were jammed with Japanese—sitting in the aisles, some of them sick, hungry, crying—returning to their country. Kitako was shocked by the unkempt appearance of some of the travelers, and how desperate and distraught people seemed. Sitting across from a group of journalists who wrote for a large Tokyo paper, Kitako finally heard how bad things were back at home, and about the details of the bombing of Pearl Harbor, and about the war with the United States. When Kitako grew visibly saddened by the news, the reporters distracted her with descriptions of their favorite coffee shops and bars and restaurants in Ginza, and they all vowed to meet up there when the war was over.

While standing in line for a boat to Kyushu, Kitako watched a young Japanese cabin boy taking bribes from the passengers as they boarded. "One mother and her children were turned away because they had no extra money, no tip for him," she says. "So when my turn in line came, I gave him an extra five yen or so, just to get onboard. I'll never forget how awful that was—to witness greed like that. It was a difficult situation and a time when people should be treating each other as kindly as possible. But here was this cabin boy sending a desperate woman and her children to the end of the line—I'm not sure they ever boarded the ship—because he didn't get a tip of a few yen."

That trip home from Manchuria changed her forever, she says. Not simply for the level of human misery and the crowded conditions, but because of how she'd seen people treating each other, the rudeness and selfishness. "Times have gotten really bad," she remembers thinking. "People have lost their grace, and their sense of respect for life and for each other."

Once in Tokyo, even with the war on, it was a wonderful comfort to be back in her old neighborhood among her friends and family. Her parents were ecstatic that she'd come home safely with their first grandchild in her arms. And they were happy that Morie, once he'd made his way back from China, had decided to remain in Tokyo at the Katos' house while he looked for work in the city, and were overjoyed when he was offered a job developing refrigeration technology—inventing a method of freezing fish on boats for a prestigious company. The offer of money was so great, it wouldn't take too long before they'd be able to afford a house of their own in Azabu, or so Kitako was told. But Morie hesitated, and eventually turned down the offer. "Aside from the fishing part, the enterprise didn't interest me too much," he says.

He liked the sound of another offer more: building and running a power plant in the rugged wilderness of Hachimantai, the far north of Japan. It was about thirty miles from Castle No. 5 Town, where he'd grown up. The job came with a big house too. He took it.

Kitako's return to the snow country in 1942 was even more jarring than her time in Manchuria. That was the most disturbing thing: the sense of dislocation she felt as soon as she stepped onto the train for the north. In Japan, she should feel at home. But each mile of the twenty-two-hour train ride took her farther and farther into a forbidding landscape and away from comfort and the people she loved. The mountains were so steep and menacing. The plains were so flat she felt that she could see to the ends of the world.

Her first years were the most difficult. She had trouble understanding the Akita dialect or appreciating the charms of country life. She heard stories about toddlers being killed by black bears or poisonous snakes and she worried about Atsuko. There were so many kinds of bugs in the summer, flying and crawling and swarming—beetles, spiders, mosquitoes, cicadas, dragonflies—she was always swatting or smashing, or kicking something away. The only time she felt victorious was when she hung netting over the beds. Mostly, though, she missed having light and power and heat. "I was so shocked to see how backward things were and the way people lived," she says. "I'd gotten used to electricity and gas in Tokyo. The snow country was like an old place from the past."

The poverty and hard life of the north were made even more dramatic by the war and rationing. It was difficult to find food, and there was almost nothing to buy in the stores—no winter shoes or coats or wool blankets. When the harsh weather came in December, Kitako was stunned to see country people wearing cotton kimonos and straw shoes in the snow.

And there was a reason it was called the snow country: There weren't just mounds of snow or piles of snow in Hachimantai. There were avalanches, fortresses, ramparts, steep towering walls of snow. In the village, the drifts were so high that children jumped out of second-story windows into them and slid down to the street. The roads closed in December or January and only the train tracks were kept clear so the locomotive could run between the remote towns.

Kitako remembers the forlorn whistle of the train in the distance. It would come and go, come again, then fade. The tracks seemed to lead to nowhere, and to nothing, from one lifeless snow country town to the next. Her second child, a boy named Moritake, was born in 1943, and Kitako felt more isolated than ever. She heard stories about two other Tokyo girls who'd moved to the north during the war and hadn't survived. They'd had nervous breakdowns and been returned to their families on stretchers. Sometimes Kitako wished that would happen to her.

"I knew nobody, and had nobody to talk to," she says. "There was no fun, no sense of gaiety." The local people didn't really seem to know how to get to know a new person, or chitchat gracefully, the way city people did. On the roads and fields, the snow country women wore white scarves covering their heads and faces—only their eyes were visible. When the winter came, the snow was lovely at first, but Kitako's world was reduced to the inside of the house and stoking the woodstove. And while one of the famous features of snow country life was the opportunity to soak outdoors in the hot springs, or *onsen,* as a way to keep warm, Morie and Kitako's house in Hachimantai was so close to an active volcano that the water of the hot springs was yellow with sulfuric acid and its gases were toxic during certain parts of the year.

Their company house was impressively large—and pretty elegant—but there was no hot water, or gas, and electricity didn't arrive until the power plant was finished two years later. Kitako did laundry by hand, cooked all the meals on a woodstove, and gathered kindling and small logs in the woods behind the house. There were twelve or so other farms in Hachimantai, but spread apart, each a small colony of life. Miles from the market, Kitako had a hard time figuring out where to get meat and fish until she became acquainted with door-to-door vendors and local farmers who sold things out of their greenhouses and root cellars. As the war went on, her worries about finding enough to eat grew more intense. Rice was impossible to come by, and meat grew scarce. It was also around that time that Morie came home with a puppy.

THE FIREBOMBING OF TOKYO began in the late winter of 1944. Kitako listened carefully for news of Azabu on the radio and was devastated to learn her old neighborhood had been struck. A report came on: Everyone in the city would be given a four-day pass to travel anywhere in Japan for free, to help evacuate Tokyo. Kitako began to make preparations in the house, expecting her mother and father and eight siblings to turn up any day. She scrounged the markets for bedding and blankets, and for extra food. For four days straight, she and Morie drove the horse cart to the station and waited for the trains from Tokyo to come in. "But on the fourth day, still nobody had come," Kitako says. "I was so worried, and heartbroken."

Eventually word reached her that her brothers and sisters were safe, and their family house remained intact. As dangerous as Tokyo was, though, nobody wanted to depart for the north. ("You didn't go to the snow country," one sister says, "unless somebody made you.") But in March of that year, the city was firebombed again, so heavily that Morie took the train down to see the devastation and help survivors. They'd heard on the radio that huge portions of residential Tokyo had been demolished. Morie arrived to find the family house partially destroyed, but all the Katos were alive. And even then, only one of Kitako's younger sisters, Mitsuko, would return with him to the north.

"I remember the train ride," Mitsuko says, "and how depressing it was. I wondered why I had agreed to go."

Morie went down to the city again in May, after more bombing, bringing back the rest of Kitako's brothers and sisters, some of whom were still in grade school—and stunned and homesick and already missing their parents, who had evacuated with other relatives to the South.

So the large house in Hachimantai filled up—twelve people in all—and Morie and Kitako's lives narrowed down to basic survival: trying to find enough food, enough bedding, enough warm clothing and heavy shoes. The village began holding bomb drills, fire drills, and the women and children were trained to fight with bamboo spears. They worked in the rice fields, too, in exchange for food. In a moment of desperation Kitako went into town and sold her two best kimonos, the ones she'd brought all the way from Tokyo in a special trunk. Her wedding kimono was one of them—an exquisite work of woven silk and golden thread. The other, an orange silk kimono with purple lilies, her parents had bought for her at Takashimaya, a fancy department store, and she'd worn it for her nineteenth birthday celebration. "Everybody was selling their kimonos," her sister Mitsuko says. The market was glutted with silk and gold, and fine rare fabrics. Kitako came home with one hundred yen, enough money to buy three days' worth of rice.

Nobody talked about the thing in the woodshed—the creature that was now eating six pounds of food a day—or said anything directly to Morie about his dog. Morie never raised the subject either. He fed it quietly, walked it quietly, and tried to keep it out of sight. Actually, he wasn't sure if his in-laws even knew about it. But they knew. They all knew. And they were speechless with disgust. You weren't supposed to feed dogs when people were starving. You weren't supposed to give dogs rice when your family got only potatoes. But Morie was seized by a sense of mission. His feeling of infatuation or love or awe for this dog was indescribable. He was compelled to keep it alive and well—as if he didn't have enough to worry about already.

At the power plant, the military had been dropping off prisoners of war—Americans and English mostly—to work as slave labor. Kitako remembers visiting the plant and being struck by how thin and bedraggled these men looked, and how hard they had to work. Later in the year, when winter came, she had a hard time looking at the prisoners. "Their clothes were in shreds. They barely had shoes," she says. "Their beards were long and their hair was greasy and matted. You've never seen people so thin," she says, "and they were forced to work outside in the cold." Kitako wondered if it was right, but never said a word to anyone, even to Morie. "I thought people would think I was unpatriotic to have thoughts like that. Those men were the enemy, after all." Their countries were dropping bombs on Japan, killing people she knew, and destroying places she loved, so that made things pretty black and white, didn't it? You weren't supposed to say compassionate things about them. But Kitako wasn't so sure.

She had known only wars and skirmishes, battles and invasions, air raids and firebombs as long as she could remember. "During my entire youth, life was tense," she says. "People focus on the war with America and the West as the only one that matters now. But for me, my entire youth had been taken up with wars. They weren't skirmishes. To us, they were real wars. I was always nervous and on guard—never feeling relaxed or carefree. Everything was so chaotic. And I remember that victory was always around the corner.

We're winning! We've almost succeeded! The official news was always upbeat."

Morie worked hard in those days, frequently traveling to other villages to make arrangements with local merchants and politicians. People were so happy to talk about the future, to think about how the water would someday flow through their dam and electricity would come and change their lives. The future was an easier place, freer and warmer, lit by wires and bright bulbs and nurtured by beautiful machines. To pass the time, Morie liked to gab about country matters, about the depth of the snowfall, or new irrigation techniques, or whether intestinal worms and other livestock diseases were under control. But no matter what, or how long it took, there was always one subject he liked above all others, and always raised: dogs. Were there any Akitas around? Who might have some?

Eventually he made a list of suspected dog owners, and after a careful investigation, done as discreetly as possible, he put together a head count of dogs. In the middle of 1945, as far as he could tell, there were only sixteen Akitas left. That's when he got to thinking: Why not try to breed a few more?

Three

Three Good Lucks

The old writings about snow country dogs say the color of their fur should be subtle, almost plain. The aim was to reflect the feeling of nature, of colors fading softly, the way a wheat field burns in autumn or snow melts into clear water.

Three Good Lucks had a rich red coat that faded quietly to gold and pale yellow—and then to white on the tip of his nose and tail. Morie used to sit for hours, drinking cups of sake and looking at the dog. Three Good Lucks embodied so many admirable qualities, so effortlessly, Morie liked to study how they came together in one single breathing animal. "I learned so much from him about the qualities of a good Akita," he says, "about the color, the bone structure, the spirit, the innocence, and the feeling of calm."

THE DAY THE EMPEROR announced Japan's surrender in August 1945, Morie came home from the power plant before lunch. He'd heard there was going to be an important national broadcast at noon and so, gathered along with Kitako and her sisters and brothers, he sat by the radio. Nine days before, the Americans had used a new kind of bomb in Hiroshima and again three days later in Nagasaki, but there was chaos and communication delays, all the news coming from the bombed-out areas was spotty and confusing. The government was still acting upbeat.

The emperor came on the radio. His voice was high, tense, and he was speaking in a days-of-yore formal manner. They'd lost the war, he said. Japan had surrendered. After years of government propaganda, of being told that victory was close at hand, the news was hard to believe, almost unimaginable. "It was the first time I'd heard the emperor speak," Morie says, "and he sounded so solemn— almost despondent. Suddenly everything had changed."

Even before the emperor finished, "we heard airplanes overhead," Kitako says. Her younger brother, who was visiting from the air base in Aomori while he waited for an assignment as a kamikaze pilot, heard a low rumbling in the sky and identified the source. "That's a B-29, a bomber," he said. "And there's more than one."

The planes were so low and loud, they could barely hear the emperor's voice anymore. Morie and Kitako walked outside the house—the sky was full of B-29s, sure enough, but bombs weren't dropping. The heavens were full of parachutes, so many different colors of them. And below each parachute, a large barrel was swinging. "They were coming down at once, hundreds of them, and seemed to be aiming for the power plant, but a few of them landed in our vegetable garden," says Kitako. "Yellow parachutes. Green parachutes. Red parachutes. There was a color code—we figured that out later. Each barrel carried supplies and food, and each color meant a different kind of supply."

Not much later, Kitako saw the detainees and prisoners of war from the power plant walking on the road to the village. "They were wearing brand new clothing," she says. "Not really uniforms but shiny gray jumpsuits, so new, and they had real shoes—boots! Their hair looked clean and it was plastered back with some kind of oil or cream. I was so impressed with how neatly they'd combed their hair, and how clean they were, and how quickly everything was happening. I couldn't believe the transformation. They walked through our village and were handing out chocolates to the children. When a soldier tried to give one to Atsuko, she was scared and ran away. So he left one for her. I remember thinking, *Who are these Americans? This is incredible.*"

FOR MORIE, THE WAR'S END meant an addition to the doghouse and a separate coop for weaned puppies. He had two full-grown Akitas—No Name and a nameless stud, now liberated from their muted log cabin life. Morie walked them in the sharp morning light, waving to neighboring farmers as he crossed their rice fields on his way to the steep mountain paths where the dogs were allowed to run off-leash.

Yamazaki came by the house frequently in those days. He was the dog merchant who had sold both dogs to Morie, and he was interested in the first litter of puppies. A close friendship had developed between the two men, the sort of bond that Morie would enjoy over the course of his life with many others, all dog people: breeders, judges, trainers, owners, vets, canine geneticists. It didn't matter how old they were, or where they'd been raised. It didn't matter whether they'd gone to college or had a decent job. What they didn't have in common seemed irrelevant in the face of what they had together. Dogs and sake. They'd drink and talk dogs. For Morie, this was a divine and irresistible combination.

The former Tokyo taxi driver was an intense man, very serious, and married to a former geisha. He and his wife had moved up north to escape the bombing, and as soon as the war ended, he got deep into dogs, eventually becoming a high-profile merchant with a reputation for selling expensive Akitas from good lines. A graceful, composed man who liked to talk, Yamazaki began stopping by Morie's house almost every day in the early evening, around drinking time. After a few cups of sake, he and Morie would weave their way to the doghouse to look at the puppies again. They were fuzzy and vigorous—painfully cute. Morie had trouble containing his joy and pride when he showed them off, but couldn't help noticing that Yamazaki refrained from effusive compliments. Did Yamazaki know something about the puppies that Morie didn't? Was there a way to tell if one of them would grow up into a fine, prizewinning Akita? Morie had theories in those days, and hunches, and stabs in the dark, but mostly, it was just good to be raising dogs. And he was pleased with the puppies that No Name and the nameless stud had produced so far. They had big bones, heavy faces, and as he likes to say, "sparkling eyes."

KITAKO'S MEMORIES OF that winter are bleaker—and don't include much about how cute the puppies were. Atsuko was four. Moritake was turning two. Kitako was twenty-five and pregnant with her third child. And after the initial relief when the war ended, almost euphoria, the winter that followed seemed the longest and darkest of all: There was even less food. Her young sisters and brothers were restless to return to the city but stayed in Hachimantai while the family house in Tokyo was rebuilt, another six or eight months. Along with Atsuko and Moritake, they were frequently cold and hungry. Rice was available, but only on the black market for exorbitant prices. And it continued to be impossible to find warm clothing and proper shoes. When a wool coat arrived from a Methodist Church charity in America—sent through Kitako's grandmother's church in Tokyo—grateful family members took turns wearing it. Finally in desperation, Kitako sewed jackets and coats from old blankets and asked a villager to teach her how to weave snow country sandals out of straw. Morie found surplus canvas from the power plant and made a school backpack for Atsuko, and then a pair of snow boots using inner tube rubber for the soles.

How solemn the days seemed, how gray and colorless, how deep the snow. "I felt so disconnected and alone," she says. "It was so bleak. It was almost as if you were afraid to laugh, or be cheerful. If you rode on the train to another town, you'd see no color or shapes or people or even houses—just a flat landscape of white. There was no vibrancy, only emptiness. There was an end-of-the-world feeling."

One afternoon Kitako went to the market in another town and, losing track of time, missed the last train back to Hachimantai. Instead of riding the two train stops, she had to walk home with her newborn baby daughter Ryoko on her back and bags of groceries in one hand. "I had a thick wool blanket that I wore—like a poncho—and I threw it around me and over Ryoko and pulled it tight across my chest and held it there, with the groceries in my other hand. I walked for miles in the snow that way. The light grew darker with each step."

By the time she reached the house, the stars were out. She had a feeling "beyond lonesomeness," she says. "It's almost indescribable.

And I remember thinking: How did I come to live in this sorrowful place—under the snow for six months of the year? I told myself, *I am just getting through all this for my children. That's all I have.*

"It's something you never forget, an experience like that," she says now. "But at the same time, all of Japan was so dark. Tokyo had turned to ashes. No one could escape a sense of loss. It wasn't just in the north. It was everywhere."

When winter finally ended, the sunshine felt golden—more powerful, almost heavy with warmth. There was a wonderful frenzy of activity that came with the fine weather that first spring after the war, as though they'd woken up to find themselves alive again. Determined that he'd never again worry about having enough food, Morie dug a root cellar as soon as the soil thawed—shoveling down four feet into the dirt floor of the kitchen and creating a large cool storage space. He built a rabbit hutch to keep rabbits for eating, and a grape arbor in a sunny spot of the garden, and he bought goats for milking.

He started work on the first of three ponds. It took weeks to dig out the hole with a shovel, and when the pond was deep enough, he filled it with mountain water and stocked it with carp and trout—so he could offer fresh sashimi to visitors when they stopped by. He cranked up production on an illegal sake-making operation too, and occasionally used *doboroku*, or home-brew alcohol made from fermented apples, to trade in town for favors and food. But they were always prepared to hide it at a moment's notice. "Because we had to be in touch with the power plant at all times, we had an alarm at the house in case of plant emergencies—like a signal," Kitako explains. "Morie made arrangements with the plant workers to sound the alarm if the tax collector was coming up our road, so we'd know to put away the bootleg sake."

At night, to entertain the family, and eventually the entire village,

Morie repaired a broken film projector and stretched a curtain across the wall of the tatami room, or formal room of the house, and showed movies. His most ingenious creation, though, was an electric coil that he rigged to a wooden box in the kitchen, providing the family with a supply of hot water. Encouraged by his success, he built a large bathtub over a woodstove in a private ground-floor room and invited the neighboring villagers of Hachimantai—seventeen or eighteen families in all—to come by and use it as much as they liked. For Japanese people, the chance to soak in a steaming hot bath was hard to refuse. Morie and Kitako had always entertained power plant employees and friends from nearby towns, but now the number of drop-by visitors became an endless parade, along with the frequent visits of Yamazaki. Morie couldn't help but notice that, with his in-laws back in Tokyo for good, the flow of guests and company put his wife in better spirits.

A natural cook, Kitako had learned to make regional country dishes like *kiritampo,* a chicken and dumpling stew that Akita prefecture is known for. With more guests than ever, she became an adventurous and resourceful chef. As a girl growing up, she'd never learned much about cooking, but now, when she found herself missing the city, and city food—there was no tempura or curry or fried chicken in the north—she experimented with her own versions and tried them out on her sisters.

When she had arrived in the snow country, she had found the locals unsophisticated and their heavy Akita accents hard to understand, but more and more, because of her growing interest in cooking and the pleasures of entertaining, she began to meet more people and even to make some friends. Asking villagers about mountain cooking and other aspects of their lives, Kitako grew to respect their cleverness and self-reliance. The farmers' wives had taught Kitako how to weave straw mats to sleep on, how to harvest garden vegetables by the first frost, how to get things jarred and pickled by the beginning of November, and how to keep daikon radishes fresh all winter by burying them just beneath the surface of the snow.

Kitako and Morie soon acquired a reputation for hospitality and generosity. Even a casual drop-in visitor was ushered first to the steaming bath, and then handed a full cup of sake—never just tea. Afterward they were invited to sit down at the table. Kitako had a firm policy: Nobody left without being given something to eat.

Dog shows started up in the spring of 1946. Morie kicked things off and hosted an informal affair at the house in Hachimantai. It wasn't a show or exhibition as much as a celebration—with Kitako's food, Morie's sake, and a gathering of dog buddies Morie had collected in his travels, or friends of Yamazaki. "We all wanted to see what we had," Morie says, "and how many Akitas there were around."

The dogs arrived one by one—there were about forty or fifty of them by that time, most of them young—and the shocking thing was how dissimilar they looked. Different sizes, and a stunning array of shapes, they barely seemed to belong to the same breed. Some of the Akitas had big mastiff heads and hulking frames. Others had loose skin that made their fur look draped over their spines. There were floppy ears, tails that didn't curl, stumpy legs. One thing they had in common: The malnutrition of the war years had left the dogs scrawny and their coats weak. Their legs were short, and bodies low to the ground. It was almost embarrassing how superior No Name looked by comparison.

A month or so later, Morie heard about a regional dog show—a real contest with prizes—and signed up, calling No Name "Yama-biko" on the entry form. His dreams of glory were so strong that he rose at midnight on the morning of the show, unable to sleep. Earlier at dinner, he'd boasted to his family about No Name's obvious champion qualities—and told them to prepare to apologize for doubting Morie over the last two years. Maybe now Kitako would see what he'd been up to, and the importance of the magnificent dog for which they'd all sacrificed.

Early the next morning, Morie loaded No Name into the wagon of the horse cart and rode in the direction of the far-off village where the dog show was being held. The long trip went quickly, Morie's head swirling with visions of his imagined destiny. Arriving at the show, he assessed the competition and felt even more encouraged. The crowd was full of the usual diehards—anybody who'd man-aged to keep a dog during the war had to be there—but their Akitas looked weak. What a ragtag group of canines, Morie thought. Floppy ears and limp tails were everywhere. Bursting with pride, Morie walked his gorgeous dog into the ring, holding the leash high in a fist over his head. While other owners fussed over their dogs and sometimes adjusted their tails to make them seem curlier, Morie ignored No Name, tried to seem aloof, almost oblivious. He didn't need to fuss over the dog or move her tail around. No Name was spectacular—and nearly perfect in every way. Anybody could see that.

Anybody but the judges. First place went to a loud, lumbering dog from Odate. No Name got second. Morie was beside himself—and found it hard to hide his anger and disappointment. All the way home in the horse cart, he fumed. Those judges were crazy. What was wrong with them? "I couldn't believe it! The whole thing was very mysterious to me. I suspected that the competition was rigged. None of those other dogs seemed any better to me."

Over the ensuing weeks, Morie spent hours and hours discussing the results of the show with Yamazaki and any family member who was willing to linger at the dinner table and listen. No Name's loss seemed like a gross injustice, an outrage, or a fluke. But after several more regional competitions in which the dog continued to take second place—never first prize—Morie's bitterness turned to paranoia and, eventually, utter befuddlement. What was wrong with the dog? Why couldn't she win? Kitako and the children were no comfort. They'd finally given her a nickname: "The Dog Who Comes in Second."

In time, Morie got an explanation from a man he respected without reservation, an older and well-educated gentleman named Masutaro Ito, who had inherited the position of *soncho,* or mayor of a nearby village. Ito was a small, understated man with a big mustache and an old world accent. He never drank, always wore a dark suit, and lived on a large estate where his family had been growing rice and keeping dogs for many generations. He'd had a kennel of dogs before the war, as well as several dog boys. On the subject of Akitas, he was the ultimate authority, as far as Morie was concerned. "Do you want to know the truth?" Ito asked him.

"Yes."

"An Akita should look rugged and imposing," Ito said. It wasn't a matter of length and height as much as heft. No Name might be pretty, and her color was lovely, but beauty wasn't enough. A dog needed to be strong, and dominate the show with a feeling of power and energy. Morie's dog hadn't done that. In fact, she looked thin and wimpy.

Morie stopped showing No Name after that. What was the point? The competitions weren't worth the trouble or heartache, and Morie didn't like the way the shows were run and crudely judged either. As time passed and he recovered from his crushing sense of disappointment, he began to see more clearly what the real problem was—not just with No Name, but with the dog shows in general: Nobody agreed on what an Akita was—or should be. Everybody had an opinion, but there was no consensus and no consistent standard. Morie could remember the snow country dogs of his childhood, how confident and healthy they were. Was it even possible to return the breed to that? After decades of cross-breeding with German shepherds and mastiffs, and after the war years, when they'd been killed off or starved, the Akita was a hodgepodge, a random assortment of traits and styles. But what was the ideal?

OVER THE CENTURIES the villages of the north, like Shimizu, where Masutaro Ito's family had raised dogs, had competed against each other in the dog ring. Each village favored a slightly different style of Akita, almost the way competing soccer teams have different colored jerseys. A village could become known for a certain color dog, or a distinct trait or personality. For instance, in snowy Iwate, the northernmost prefecture of Honshu, where the dogs were bred largely for tracking and bear hunting, a lean dog with stamina and good predatory instincts prevailed. And in the city of Odate, a longtime center of dog fighting, the dogs were muscular, stocky, and stoic—all traits that grew out of the old fighting dog breeding stock for which Odate had been famous. In fact, the brave dogs of Odate were so legendary that until 1927 when the breed's name was officially established as the Akita, it was called *Odate inu,* or Odate dog.

In the early twentieth century, as dog fighting became unpopular— seen as barbaric and outlawed in some regions—the same villages competed for dominance at dog shows. The exhibitions were essentially beauty and charisma pageants but seemed to engender great antagonism, as if the hostility of the bloody dog fights had to find expression somewhere. No rivalry was uglier or more deep-rooted than the one between Odate and Akita City, the two largest cities in Akita prefecture. The judges took sides, unfortunately, and in the early competitions, if there was a majority of judges from Odate at a show, then the best dog in the stocky Odate style—called the "Dewa" style—would win. When most of the judges came from Akita City or its surrounding villages, the leaner style of the "Ichinoseki" line prevailed.

Then, in the late 1940s, two dogs were born—two spectacular Akitas that embodied the ideals of each of these bloodlines so magnificently that the age-old rivalry between Odate and Akita City began to intensify and sharpen. And it wasn't long before the entire northern dog world was forced to choose a side.

Kongo was a great beauty with the strong, muscular body and dynamic shape that were the hallmarks of the Dewa line. His spine was straight and long. His chest was barrel-shaped. His coat color was *kurogoma,* or black sesame, the tips of his fur were black against a lighter brown undercoat. He had a striking, intelligent, shepherd-like face as well as several other qualities which were viewed as attractive although vaguely associated with Western dogs: soft ears, loose skin, and wrinkles around the muzzle. His tail didn't curl tightly, but sort of swooped to one side.

If Kongo was an alluring creature, his owner, Hiroko Abe, a former actress with a penchant for self-promotion, was even more so. As Kongo began to garner national prizes in the late 1940s, Abe's husband, Yutaka Abe, a Tokyo movie producer, collaborated with Hikashi Hashimoto, a famous dog dealer and handler, devising a

昭和 28 年 9 月 1 日発行 第2巻 第9号 臨時増刊昭和 27 年 2 月 20 日第三種郵便物認可 昭和 26 年 12 月 24 日 国鉄承認雑誌第 号

日本犬大観

A Manual of The Japanese Dog.

愛犬の友臨時増刊

國宝犬金剛号

Kongo

national marketing plan for the dog. Kongo was photographed with glamorous Hiroko for a series of posters and advertisements, proclaiming the dog as the greatest Akita of all time. The fact that women didn't routinely appear in advertisements in Japan at that time, much less to promote themselves or their dogs, gained Kongo even more notice. Another population began to take notice of the champion too: dog-loving American GIs, thousands of whom were now stationed throughout Japan.

As Kongo was becoming a national celebrity, another dog entered the scene—very quietly at first. He came to embody another set of ideals and dreams about what an Akita should be, and would eventually become Kongo's archrival.

Descended from an old line of hunting dogs in the far north, Goromaru embodied the best qualities of the Ichinoseki line. His legs were longer and his body was less stocky than Kongo's, giving him the appearance of lean strength. His coloring was unusual—a red pinto coat with a white blaze on his chest, a black mask, and a white nose. Rather than resembling that of a shepherd, Goromaru's head was roundish, more like a bear's. And unlike Kongo, whose skin was loose, Goromaru's was tight, almost as though it had been closely upholstered to his body. To add to the feeling of tautness, his tail curled perfectly into a circle, his face was unwrinkled, his eyes small, and his ears pricked and alert.

Goromaru's owner was a well-known fixture in the dog world of the north, a man named Funakoshi. Unlike Kongo's glamorous and social owners, Funakoshi was a serious man who didn't care for marketing and self-promotion. An idealist, and a Communist, his goal was to infuse the traditional dogs of the north with lasting good traits. He wasn't bent on cultivating dogs of a certain size or beauty, or even those with excellent hunting skills. Funakoshi had a comprehensive

Goromaru

list of qualities that he claimed to be breeding for—and hoped to see validated by competition. When he talked about dogs, it wasn't about today's dog or tomorrow's litter. He took the long view, and his ultimate goals for the breed dangled in the far-off future.

From the beginning, as much as Morie was impressed by Kongo, he preferred Goromaru. He had his own pro–Akita City bias that dated to childhood, and also, No Name shared a common ancestor with Goromaru. But what began as a rather gentle preference on Morie's part became more fervent after he and Kitako traveled to a big show and saw Goromaru in the flesh. "I remember how heavy and impressive his paws were," Kitako says. "He had great stature and a really impeccable taut feeling to his body," gushes Morie. "There was no looseness. He looked ready to fight an enemy at any moment—always on guard."

It happened that Masutaro Ito was acquainted with Funakoshi, and when he heard Morie and Kitako's opinions of Goromaru, he offered to take them to meet the dog's owner. "In those days, Communists were looked upon as criminals in Japan and under scrutiny," Morie says, "but it was hard not to admire Funakoshi." He was low-key and serious, and his work seemed more about love than money—something in particular that really impressed Morie, who'd come to dislike the commercial swirl around Kongo. "Whenever Goromaru would win prizes, there was so much jealousy and badmouthing among the Odate clan," Morie says. "They were hypercompetitive, and spoke so badly of Goromaru, saying the dog had weak paws and other things. I never liked that. They just wanted to have their pinup dog to promote and make money off of, so Kongo was it. He was turned into a celebrity dog to help sales."

The history of any dog breed is rife with tales of infighting and warring factions—and splits between clubs and bloodlines. Before the standards of a breed are fixed and certain clubs are recognized, there's a great deal to hash out. But in the postwar years in Japan, when so much of life was being questioned and redefined, the Kongo-versus-Goromaru rivalry and their respective bloodlines, eventually described as the Dewa and Ichinoseki lines, came to represent distinct political, philosophical, and even spiritual schools of thought. Goromaru's owner was a high-minded Communist, outspoken in his opposition to the marketing and national promotion of dogs; he preached that such practices would result in weak dogs and unethical behavior. In Odate, on the other hand, where the business of dogs had been established for generations and was a natural part of everyday life, it seemed ludicrous not to take advantage of financial opportunities. What was so awful about wanting to sell Kongo's offspring for the highest price?

Amid the confusion and noisy infighting, Morie noticed that something positive was happening: "For the first time there were pictures of two very different dogs to look at—Kongo and Goromaru—and people began to talk seriously about traits, finally studying each part of the Akita. The nose. The face. The tail. The coat."

And at a time when money was scarce, and the profits from a dog show victory could keep a family fed, the dog world became a lucrative but rather brutal marketplace, no matter what side of the Akita debate you were on. Dogs were often sold as soon as they won a title. Puppies went to the highest bidders. There were stories of dog kidnappings, falsified papers, even poisonings of rivals. Morie was happy to have stayed away from competition in those years. "It was really a struggle among dog merchants."

Morie doesn't like to talk about the other reason he stayed home and didn't enter his dogs in competition in the years following 1947. It's too difficult to discuss. Kitako had given birth to the couple's fourth child the year before, their second son. But in the winter of 1947, when he was one year old, the baby died of pneumonia. "He didn't have a fever and he was still breast-feeding, so we thought he couldn't be so sick," Kitako says. When the boy was found in bed, lifeless, Morie flew into the room and began slapping him on the cheeks to wake him up. Then, when the boy still didn't respond, Morie lifted him into the air by his feet and shook him upside down while Atsuko and Ryoko watched. "Wake up! Wake up!" Morie yelled. "Why won't you wake up?"

Not long afterward, another baby was born—a little girl. Kitako was more vigilant when the baby came down with a respiratory infection in the harsh winter of 1949, two years after the death of their second son. As soon as the girl ran a fever, and began wheezing, Kitako called for the doctor on the signal phone. "The house was cold, just too cold," Kitako says now. "I waited and waited for the doctor that time, but we lived so far out in the countryside, it took him too long. By the time he pulled up to the house in a horse cart, she was already dead."

Morie and Kitako fought a great deal in the months afterward, so loudly that it was sometimes hard for the children to remain in the same room. Morie drank more than ever. And Kitako grew more vocal about her frustration over living so far from anything, village or town or other families. How many hours had she waited for the doctor? How would she keep the rest of the children alive?

Morie ignored her, or appeared to. But not long afterward he bought his first car—a black 1948 Mazda with three wheels. It had a small engine, just 360 cubic centimeters, but in good weather it made decent time on the bumpy dirt roads of Hachimantai. And maybe, with some good luck, the doctor would never be too late again.

. . .

IN THE SPRING following that dark winter, Masutaro Ito arrived at the house one morning with a handsome red puppy in his arms. As always, Ito was understated and dignified, explaining that he was just "dropping off" a dog to strengthen Morie's kennel, but there was a sense that the older man was offering something more.

The puppy had clean lines and a strong build. The color of his red coat was deep and strong, yet faded beautifully to a pale orange and white. As spectacular as he was physically, the most unusual thing was his temperament, especially for a puppy. Morie noticed it immediately. The dog was calm and confident, and seemed enormously happy—as if basking in his own warm wonderful energy. Just investigating the garden, and sniffing the spring air, he seemed to fill the world with optimism.

Kitako was drawn to him, too, picking him up and carrying him around while murmuring sweet sounds. Morie had never seen her like that—so taken with an animal. Later that night, she asked if she might give him a name. It wasn't right for this dog not to have one. She wanted to call him:

Three   Good Lucks

"When you'd look at him or say his name, he made a connection with you," Kitako says. "You could sense his intelligence and spirit.

You felt you really knew him. And he really knew you—and what you'd been through."

Morie's youngest sister Haru remembers visiting Hachimantai that year, and being impressed by several things. When asking directions, she remembers the way the townspeople in Hachimantai spoke about her brother and his wife, with great respect and gratitude. And she was impressed by the size of the sprawling *bakemono,* or monster house, in which her brother's family was living. Kitako kept things so tidy and clean, and cut flowers and beautifully arranged tree branches and pines decorated the formal rooms. During the war things had been so bleak and depressed, and continued to be in most places in the snow country, yet her brother seemed to be living prosperously in a fine house with pottery and scrolls and flowers. The cedar post—an architectural detail of a traditional Japanese house that indicates the wealth and status of its owners in the formal room—was "so thick that I couldn't put my arms around it," Haru says.

Even more memorable, next to the post, in the *tokonoma*—the alcove in which a Japanese family might put a treasured scroll or shrine, and where it would have been highly improper to put your feet—there was a red dog sitting in his crate. "A dog!" Haru says. "It was unthinkable!"

Three Good Lucks didn't like the cold, Kitako explains, "and he was more sensitive than the others." She lobbied Morie to allow the dog inside, she says, because he was calmer and more people-oriented than the other dogs.

According to Morie, the cold had nothing to do with the decision to keep the dog inside. Three Good Lucks lived in the house in a kennel tucked inside the *tokonoma* because he was absolutely the finest puppy that Morie had ever owned—or might ever own. "He was simply too valuable," Morie says, "too precious, and too rare, and too special, to be left alone outside where anything could happen."

With the dog inside, Morie could check on him—drop in and have a glass of sake and just look at Three Good Lucks. There was something incredibly encouraging about him, almost inspiring. "Unless you have the chance to live with a great dog," Morie says, "you might never know what makes them so different. And how to recognize their special qualities."

Good physical traits were pretty obvious. If you trained your eye to look carefully enough, you could make drawings of dogs, and their shapes, and come to understand what was desirable. As for the coat, you could feel the dog's fur and how thick it was. You could measure the dog's length and height, and weigh him on a scale. Morie did those things with all his dogs. What you could see with your eyes, or feel with your hands—those things were easy. But the inner qualities of a great dog were much more difficult to quantify. Some of the old Akita books contained eloquent discussions about the personality or "nature" that one should seek in a dog. The traits of "elegant simplicity" and "composure" were thought to be important in an Akita, as well as grace, dignity, strength, heroism, vigor, and agreeable temperament.

Yet, Three Good Lucks seemed to have every single desirable inner quality—and to Morie this was the most wondrous and improbable thing. He was agile and moved with grace. He was stoic, and rarely whined or complained. He seldom barked, never cowered. And when the children cried, he sat beside them. When he was let off-leash in the mountains, the dog bounded away with enthusiasm but never wandered too far. The minute he was called for, he returned—happily.

Rather than quoting poems or old Akita books, Morie wanted to find a simpler way to define and express the essential thing about

Three Good Lucks in the sun and snow

Three Good Lucks that made him stand apart, aside from physical beauty and strength—things that were easy to spot. There had to be one concept that could cover all the ground, one expression that could be used to define an ideal, if only in Morie's mind. Eventually, he came up with something. He decided that Three Good Lucks had *kishō*.

気 性

Ki means spirit. *Shō* means personality or disposition. Together, as Morie interprets the characters, these two ideas mean: vitality, good energy, good instincts, intelligence, alertness. "It's a personality trait, a kind of strength and life force," Morie says. "These inner qualities are less easy to pinpoint, but you can see them if you look carefully in a dog's eyes—and study a dog's reactions to the world."

Inspired by the dog's excellence, Morie worked diligently with Three Good Lucks during his first year, frequently asking Ito's advice about how to properly raise a young dog. Ito was a believer in hearty exercise for puppies, as a way to encourage a muscular body in maturity. And Ito was a believer in a healthy diet, including plenty of calcium to promote bone size and strength. So Three Good Lucks was exercised vigorously, given long runs in the woods and mountains, fed steamed vegetables and fish heads that had large quantities of calcium to develop his bones. And at the recommendation of Ito, Morie even hired a dog boy to help out.

As Three Good Lucks reached maturity, the sweet red dog became only better and stronger—the embodiment of a rugged, loyal, gung-ho, snow-country-type dog that Morie had long admired. Returning to the show ring after a hiatus of three years, Morie's

Trophy stand at the big show

opinion of the dog was confirmed. The first time he competed, Three Good Lucks won first prize, and Morie brought home a solid bronze vessel in the shape of an ancient Greek drinking cup.

At the next show, he won again, and then again. Every time Morie went into the ring with Three Good Lucks, he brought home first prize. He lined up the drinking cups on the shelf of the *tokonoma* next to the dog's bed.

Morie talked of little else. Every small change in the dog's schedule was considered, and every change in his diet and routine. When Morie returned from an exhibition and sat around the dinner table to analyze the results over a few glasses of home-brewed sake, this time he noticed that Kitako seemed pleased to stay and listen.

The day before a major dog exhibition in Odate—speculation among the dog crowd was that Three Good Lucks would win again—Morie gave specific instructions to the dog boy that Three Good Lucks would need a good workout in the early evening. This would make the next morning's drive to the show easier and also relax the dog for competition. But when the dog boy returned to the house after a long run, Three Good Lucks appeared to be sick.

Kitako brought the dog onto her lap, and called Morie on the signal phone. "I felt so helpless," says Kitako. "In those days, there was very little you could do when a dog got sick—no animal hospitals or things like that, or shots."

At first Morie blamed himself—worried that the dog had been exercised too vigorously. But as the night wore on, and Three Good Lucks grew desperately ill and listless, Morie concluded that the dog had been poisoned, possibly by a rival dog owner. He'd heard of this kind of thing happening before.

The dog didn't bark the way other Akitas sometimes do before dying. Three Good Lucks stayed on his side with one paw touching

Three Good Lucks' grave marker

Morie's arm and his head resting in Morie's hand. Kitako sat nearby. And when it was over, Morie began to cry in a way Kitako had never seen before. "He was inconsolable," she says. It was as if all the losses of the last few years had fallen upon him at once.

The next morning, still distraught and unable to speak, Morie took the body of the dog to a skinner in a nearby village. He wanted to preserve the dog's pelt, he said. He wanted to be able to hold it in his hands and remember the color and sensational thick quality of the fur.

Morie didn't come home after that. "He was gone for three days," Kitako says. When he returned, pale and quiet and bleeding sweat, she suspected he'd been drinking. She didn't ask. She never asked. "I didn't need to know the details," she says now, "because I knew how he felt."

Morie dug a grave deep in the woods, and carved a tombstone out of cedar. It was five feet tall and elegant, with the characters of the dog's name and date of death. Afterward there was a meal at the house that Kitako says she "prepared in sadness." There would be many more beautiful dogs to come, but no Akita would live inside the house again.

"We saw lots of nasty things during that time—greed, lying, and cheating," says Morie, "and other poisonings too. But the lesson I learned is that it's better to be the one who is cheated than to be somebody who cheats. And I still believe that."

Four

Reversal Dogs

Nobody is saying that Homan wasn't a good dog. He was healthy and vigorous—and fun-loving—but his eyes were always sad and his ears looked like a bat's and his coat was baggy no matter how hard he was exercised. Morie had a string of peculiar dogs that were all descended from Three Good Lucks. They were reversal dogs—and had some undesirable traits, things the other Akita breeders were trying to eliminate in their dogs. But Morie loved them, believed in them. Or he believed in where they were heading.

Morie had a dream dog in his head, a vision of what he hoped to produce someday: a sturdy, mountain-worthy dog that carried the traits and temperament of an old-style snow country dog. It would be rough but gentle, independent but obedient, a hunter who was also thick-coated and gorgeous. But producing a great dog wasn't as easy as it looked when you were breeding Akitas. You could put two beautiful dogs together and create a lot of ugly ones. And two spirited hunters could produce a lazy creature that would rather sit in the kennel all day and watch the flies buzz.

With each litter, Morie began to discover that every dog had obvious traits and subtle traits, and then it had secret traits that lay like puzzle pieces in a locked box. When you breed dogs, the box is unlocked and the puzzle pieces find their mates. The unseen becomes seen. Quiet things roar. And something new is created.

DOG FEVER OVERTOOK the snow country in the early 1950s, a strange frenzy for dogs, almost madness. Unlike the old days, when Morie would travel for work and raise the subject of dogs, hoping somebody would humor him, he had become a magnet for would-be dog breeders. People gravitated to him—wanting advice, asking questions. They showed up at his house on bicycles with empty baskets, looking for puppies to buy. Morie was almost sick of the subject. Dogs, dogs, dogs. Everybody wanted to know where he got his, how much they ate, whether he had puppies to sell, and by the way, did he charge a stud fee?

Akitas were the answer to everybody's problems in those days, because they had all heard some ridiculous, impossible story about how much an American serviceman had paid for a puppy.

Americans were dog lovers, it turned out—loved to walk them, loved to play with them, loved to give them this bad-smelling canned food instead of kitchen scraps like fish heads and rice. Morie heard Americans let their dogs sleep in bed with them. That couldn't be true. He heard they trained their dogs to do circus tricks, like shaking hands and dancing. Who cares if a dog can dance? He didn't know any Americans, and had only heard the stories, but from what he gathered they were so enthusiastic about snow country dogs—so completely besotted with Akitas—it was hard to be critical.

Morie's complaints, as usual, lay mostly with his countrymen. He couldn't help noticing that the same farmers who had clubbed their dogs to death and sold the pelts during the war were now enchanted by the breed that they had helped to almost wipe out. The greed was hard to fathom. With puppies in the back of their wagons, they were heading up to Misawa Air Base in Aomori prefecture, where tens of thousands of airmen were stationed, and selling any dog they had— anything with fur and four legs—and for the most amazing prices. During the war, Misawa had been an imperial base where kamikaze pilots were trained and left for their missions. Now, after being bombed and rebuilt, it was loaded with lonely American servicemen who were buying dogs. "Suddenly everybody was a dog breeder," Morie says, "and every dog was an Akita."

The dog sellers returned from Misawa with tales that were hard to believe. The Americans seemed to think even the mangiest Akita was the most miraculous creature in existence, heartier than a husky, braver than Lassie. They described their new Akitas as acutely intelligent, almost extrasensory. They'd never seen a dog so conscientious and tidy either—their Akitas cleaned and groomed themselves after eating, the way a cat would. (Morie laughed: Didn't all dogs do that?) More than anything, they loved the breed's loyalty. Japanese sometimes referred to the Akita as *ikken isshu*, or one-person dog, because it focused on its owner with single-minded intensity. Morie remembered his own experiences in the military. As a young man stationed on a minesweeper patrolling the Yangtze River in China, he'd nearly died—had been blasted out of his ship by an exploding mine and floated for days on the river, waiting to be rescued. How alone he felt . . . and scared. He sympathized with servicemen in a strange country, and could imagine how they'd find a dog's devotion and companionship comforting, even magically so.

The Akita was virtually nonexistent in the West. As far as anybody knew, Helen Keller was the only American who had owned one—and this seemed to be another ingredient in Americans' fascination with the breed. Keller was an enormous celebrity in the States, and a woman who had transcended her own blindness and deafness by the force of her spirit and intelligence. With all that going for her, it was hard to imagine she could be wrong about a dog.

Keller's two Akitas had come from Odate and shared the same bloodlines as Kongo, which only helped the aggressive marketing campaign pitched to Americans that was already under way. When Keller returned to Japan in 1948 and thanked the city of Odate for its superb dogs, nothing could have been sweeter for the Kongo bloodlines. Two years later, the Japanese government made things even better for the Odate dogs. Kongo received a newly created award: In addition to being a national champion, he was a *kokuhō*, or living national treasure, one of the highest honors bestowed in Japan. The dog was of such historical and cultural importance, he was now officially protected—and not allowed to leave the country.

In the old days of the snow country, nobody relied on bloodlines much. The observable qualities of a dog—how it performed in the fighting ring or show ring, or as a hunter—was the main thing, not its pedigree. The Akita Preservation Society (AKIHO) kept a register of bloodlines, but since the snow country dogs roamed freely before the war, and mated indiscriminately, the notion of pedigrees was suspect, almost something to make jokes about. But all that had changed. Increasingly valuable, Akitas were now kept in pens and kennels, and mating was carefully supervised.

Kongo wasn't allowed to leave the country, but his offspring sure did. Dewa dogs were popular and sold for the most money all over Japan in the early 1950s, but especially at American bases. Buying into a champion bloodline was an established concept in the West, but also, the dogs in the Dewa style had a look that the Americans had come to expect in an Akita from all the posters they'd seen of Kongo: a long shepherd's snout, a muscular body and black mask. While some dogs lived on the U.S. military bases, where they were kept as pets, others accompanied sailors and soldiers home. As the occupation troops began to return to the United States after their tour of duty was over, quite a few came back with an Akita in tow.

What were dogs selling for? Five hundred yen, one thousand yen, ten thousand yen . . . and climbing. In 1950, stud fees for Kongo or his champion son, Kincho-go, were published in the Akita Preservation Society journal at fifty thousand yen. Even with intense breeding efforts between 1948 and 1952, when the foundation stock for the modern Akita was produced in the heyday of Kongo and Goromaru, they were still relatively rare dogs. The demand was great, the supply small. And the price for a good Akita with Kongo bloodlines exceeded, in some cases, the annual salary of a snow country farmer or a carpenter or grocer. The price of two dogs could exceed the salary of a certain power plant executive too. "Money was all people talked about in those days," Morie says. "They'd gone so long with so little."

If a snow country farmer wasn't getting rich from selling Akitas, at least he was able to keep his family fed in a time when food continued to be scarce or expensive and a black market for rice and everything else was thriving. Compared to labor-intensive work, dog breeding seemed fairly easy too. Morie felt sympathetic to the poor farmers who were just trying to stay afloat; on the other hand, puppy mills had sprung up all over Akita prefecture and were churning out dogs with very little attention to quality and overall health. "Nobody knew what they were doing," Morie says. "Carpenters were giving up carpentry. Rice farmers gave up the farm. Suddenly everybody had a litter to sell."

Kitako encouraged him to sell a few puppies now and again, even to simply offset the costs of his dog habit, but Morie resisted. Every time he tried to put a price on one of his dogs, he felt uneasy. He had only one litter a year, sometimes two, and he liked to see the puppies go off to people he knew and respected. He might repay a favor or a vague social debt by giving away a puppy, and he didn't mind making an instant friend, either, but when he thought about selling a dog to a total stranger—or taking cash for a puppy—something inside him was revolted. He wasn't exactly sure why. Maybe he just didn't want to become like everybody else, and have his motivations questioned, or worse, the quality of his dogs. Kitako had trouble understanding. But maybe Morie wasn't very good at explaining his feelings, either. He hardly understood them himself.

When he looked around at his old dog buddies who had become professional breeders, all the joy seemed to have gone from their lives. Almost to a person, they had changed—soured and hardened. "They were almost insane with greed," Morie says. Yamazaki's whole life had crumbled. "As soon as he became a successful breeder, his pure love for dogs vanished." From Morie's perspective, when Yamazaki lost his pure love, he lost everything—"and made being rich look worse than being poor." And then Yamazaki's marriage fell apart. "I saw so many families broken up over the money they made," Morie says. "Dog money was like lottery winnings. It made people act crazy."

. . .

KITAKO IS NOT SURE why she worried about money and Morie never did. Maybe it was because she had been raised in the city and had certain expectations. Maybe she just worried out of habit—as if worrying was what her mind did on its own. She enjoyed having money, unlike Morie, who didn't appear to respect it or enjoy it. He seemed to regard it as unclean. He came home from the power plant every week and handed his salary to her—a thick wad of banknotes—as though he couldn't wait to get it out of his pocket. Kitako put it away, and then played a game to see how far she could make it last. She bought all the food, the necessities for the house, and the children's clothing that she wasn't able to sew herself.

Kitako wasn't a hoarder. She was just as generous as Morie when it came to sharing what she had with others. But she saw how things came and went, how fuel was collected and consumed, how kindling and logs smoked and burned in the stove and turned to ash, and how the food vanished on the plates. The children were growing bigger and eating more. The dogs were eating more. Morie was drinking more—the pantry was always full of empty sake bottles. The rice farmer delivered bags of rice. The apple farmer arrived with his linen sack of apples. The mushroom farmer came down from the mountain and sold shiitake. Kitako paid them, and traded with them, and stockpiled, and then she looked around and there was an empty rice sack, one rotten apple, and no more dried mushrooms. Things came. Things went. The cellar always needed filling up. And there was always somebody else who was hungry.

Morie was running four power plants by then, and traveling

Kitako fed the dogs

more. But during his days off in those years, he kept busy with projects around the house and either avoided Kitako or tried to stay out of her way. He improved the hot water heater that he had invented, and worked on creating a system of pipes to move the water into other rooms of the house besides the kitchen. Outdoors, he pried up tree stumps and turf for Kitako to burn. He dug a deeper pond for the carp—running an underground pipe that sloped from the kitchen to the pond so Kitako could keep a flow of scraps to feed the fish.

After installing a generator in the house, he came up with an idea for a self-heating bathtub that was based on the design of the hot water heater. Instead of putting an electric warming coil in a box or tank, he put one at the bottom of a deep bathtub. You had to float above the coil so you wouldn't get burned by it, but the water stayed hot—very hot—and the family and all the drop-by guests could bathe as much as they liked without Kitako's having to continually stoke the fire under the tub. People came from all over Hachimantai to marvel at the self-heating tub and try it out, but after one of Morie's nephews was nearly electrocuted one night, everybody was warned: Throw something in the bathwater first. "If you hear a zapping sound," Morie said, "don't get in."

Kitako's last baby was born in 1950—a skinny boy who was lively and good natured. He was exuberant, and laughed a lot. He was named Mamoru, and of all the children, he seemed to have inherited Morie's affection for animals. As soon as he could walk, the boy was draped around one of Morie's dogs. And as soon as he was walking, he was chasing puppies and getting lost in the mountains. His older sisters Atsuko and Ryoko shared the duty of looking after him. "He was very skinny and very quick—ran very fast," remembers Atsuko. "We were always looking for him."

By the time they were four or five years old, the children had duties and chores around the house. They helped with laundry— pumped the water by hand, scrubbed the clothes in a tub and wrung them and put them on a line to dry. The children gathered kindling for the woodstove and they fed the goats, chickens, and caged rabbits that Morie had behind the house. "When we were little," says Ryoko, "we were with the animals all the time, and took care of them. When we turned ten, my father said we were ready to walk the dogs—and no matter how hard they pulled the leash, you couldn't let go. After a while, it makes you pretty strong."

Without a playground or movie theater in town—or even another family close by—friends and visitors were always urged to come, and then kept around as long as possible. After ten years in the snow country, Kitako had become an enviable chef with a repertoire of regional dishes made with fresh mountain vegetables and preserved things marinated in salty miso. "Our house was always stormed by colleagues and employees, neighbors, school friends and dog friends," Kitako says. "In those days before television, there wasn't much to do for entertainment. The men just talked and drank. Or people sat around the table and ate. All I did was cook and cook and cook."

When the principal of the village school offered Kitako a job teaching—due to a shortage of teachers, he felt it might be possible to arrange for the teaching degree that she'd earned in Tokyo to be made valid in Akita prefecture—Morie told her to refuse the offer. "I make enough money already," he said. And besides, without a gas stove or gas heating until 1954, Kitako's daily life was spent overseeing the stoking of the woodstove. Without a refrigerator until the mid-1960s, she battled to make sure perishables were eaten in time, burying food in snow, storing it in the root cellar or the bottom of the well. Every morning, she cooked rice in two big pots. By bedtime, it would be gone. "All my kitchen pots were so big," Kitako says, "pans, pots, and racks—like a restaurant would have." Without Kitako at home all day, how would the rice get made? How would everything else get done?

Did Morie really make enough money? Kitako wasn't so sure. The dogs ate so much. And Morie bought nice leashes for them, and paid entry fees for the shows. The whole family had made sacrifices for the dogs, without question. But more than money, or even a teaching job, Kitako dreamt of the day she might return to the city. She dreamt of seeing her parents; they seemed to have gotten old suddenly. She dreamt of seeing her sisters—they were marrying and getting their own places in Tokyo and having their own families. She dreamt of walking on sidewalks, hearing the sounds of buses and street vendors. She dreamt of window shopping, running into friends, afternoons in coffee shops and evenings in restaurants. She dreamt of raising her children away from the mountains with their spiders and flying beetles and poisonous snakes, and where there was nothing to do but climb trees or play with puppies that would soon be given away. What kind of people would they become after growing up in the sticks? Mitsubishi sometimes made noises about sending Morie elsewhere, or to another division of its now vast network. Morie was a talented man with significant prospects and he often spoke of wanting to have another adventure. After ten years in Hachimantai, Kitako was increasingly hopeful that another adventure might come—preferably one that didn't include mountain life, or living anywhere cold.

But would Morie ever take a job in Tokyo? He had never felt comfortable in the city. His heart was really in the mountains, and the alpine groves and high meadows, the birch forests and white woods. More than anything, it was with the dogs—even more, it seemed, than with her or the children. There wasn't any point in resisting the truth. With the family, Morie was old-fashioned, very old Japan. He was stern, his expectations were high, his emotions restrained, and he was dismissive just as often as he was patient and respectful. With the dogs, everything was far easier and less complicated. He hugged them openly, talked to them sweetly. As much as he might love her, and love the children, and love his work—which he certainly did—his time with the dogs was the thing he loved most. He never tried to hide it. The dogs were like an island to which Morie floated, a pure land, a sanctuary, a place to restore himself. They were his passion, his religion. "All our friends knew—everyone who came to the house," she says. "If they asked Morie about the dogs, he'd light up—get in a good mood. We even made jokes about it."

No matter how cold the winter day was, how deep the snow, he jumped out of bed in the morning and wrapped himself in layers of clothes and scarves and caps, then put on his boots and burst from the house with enthusiasm. He released the dogs from their kennels and it was like a reunion of long lost friends. Kitako watched out the window of the house sometimes, her eyes following her husband as he led the dogs away on leashes, down into the valley, across the white fields, and up into the snowy mountains for a run.

He went on birthdays, holidays, Christmas, New Year's—no matter the weather or the day, no matter how much he'd had to drink the night before. And when he wasn't with the dogs or talking about them, Morie wasn't quite the same. His eyes stopped shining and his face went slack. If the family was sitting around the dinner table and talking about things besides mountain stuff, or country stuff, things that weren't connected in some way to the dogs, Morie would get up and leave the room. Kitako would hear the kitchen door slide open, and slide shut. And then she'd hear the dogs greeting her husband, the way she never did. Hello, Morie! Hello! Hello!

. . .

MORIE WAS AMBIVALENT about having a dog boy. The truth was, he wished he could do all those things himself—run and exercise the dogs at dawn, and feed and groom them, and run them again in the early evening. If you really loved your dogs, what was the point in hiring somebody else to take care of them? Every morning that Morie wasn't able to walk into the mountains was a lost day. And every evening that he couldn't come home to Kitako's warm kitchen and have a glass of sake, a cigarette, and take a long walk with the dogs before a hot bath, was a rather sad night.

He was traveling more than ever, between the four plants, and also attending conferences and shows as a judge with the Akita Preservation Society. On a new motorbike with a 500cc engine, Morie strapped a big basket to the saddle so a dog could ride with him. He loved zooming along the dirt roads and highways of the snow country that way—"I was always in high spirits, driving fast," he says. And if he got pulled over by the local police for speeding, "I always pointed to the dog and said, 'This is a national treasure!' and he'd let me go."

Another advantage of his honorary position as a judge, and the work travel, was that Morie was in constant touch with the dog grapevine. He knew who was raising Akitas, and where the litters were born. He made a point of trying to see all the new puppies that he could. He was trying to learn how to predict which puppies would turn into great dogs—and he kept his observations in a journal. When he'd see some promising pups, he liked to return and see them a few months later, examining them again as they matured. Visiting with other dog owners, he liked to listen to their observations and collected lots of anecdotal evidence. Morie called it "dog wisdom," even though much of it was nonsense.

Every so often, Morie came across a dog that had something different about him—a unique quality that Morie could sense intuitively. Every dog had an atmosphere of its own, and a look, and a balance of qualities as well as vulnerabilities and mannerisms that Morie found fascinating. Sometimes when he admired a dog's strengths, he tried to imagine what would happen if it were bred with one of his own. People who've never done it tend to imagine dog breeding is simple. But Morie spent untold hours contemplating the possibilities—always hopeful and excited. Life was full of mystery and magic, and risks. Genetics most of all. If you put two dogs from the same established breed together, they would reproduce themselves almost perfectly. But if you put two Akitas together, the force of the unknown took over. Beneath the obvious traits of each Akita, there were dozens of hidden ones waiting to come to the surface.

One autumn an apple farmer named Kurosawa tried to give Morie his dog. Kurosawa was busy with the apple harvest, he said, and the dog was too spirited and causing lots of headaches on the farm. The dog had a bottomless appetite too, and the farmer groused that he was going broke just trying to keep him satisfied. Would Morie be interested in taking him?

Morie didn't want the dog, to be honest. It looked like a pure Akita, but so darn ugly. Who'd want an ugly Akita like that? But feeling badly for the farmer, Morie agreed to keep the dog until the harvest was over. Morie took him home and put him in a pen. Realizing the fence around the pen was too low, Morie tied a heavy chain to the dog's collar—until a taller enclosure could be built—and tied the chain to a steel fence.

The next morning, the pen was empty. Kurosawa's dog had

Morie with Kurosawa-Tora

broken the heavy chain and run back to the apple orchard. It was such an amazing, Houdini-like stunt that Morie carried the cut chain into the village to show everybody. "The dog became very famous for this—all over Hachimantai," Morie says, "and we started calling him Kurosawa-Tora." Kurosawa is the name of the apple farmer. 虎 Tora means "tiger."

"He was a really bad-looking dog," Morie says, "but obviously had some impressive traits. He had a certain *kishō* that my dogs were lacking at that time. So I brought Kurosawa-Tora home with me for a while, and he became the father of some very strong puppies."

A dog didn't have to be beautiful to be spectacular. And a dog didn't need a fine pedigree either. As much as Morie had studied canine genetics during the eight years that he'd been breeding dogs, Morie relied just as much on bits of snow country wisdom and his gut instinct about all animals. They were full of secrets. You had to be poised for surprises. Morie found it humorous that suddenly all the cousins of Kongo were bringing in astronomical prices, and so many people were jumping on the Kongo bandwagon, as if creating more national treasures were going to be an easy feat.

The fact that a dog had a famous father or grandfather didn't mean too much. And after Three Good Lucks died, Morie struggled to create another red dog as marvelous as he was. He bred all of his puppies that he could get his hands on. And then he bred the offspring of those puppies. But no red dogs came, only Homan—in 1952.

Homan was a large, lumbering Akita with a strong body and lots of vigor. He was fun-loving, energetic, bright, and devoted. Morie liked him enormously—as soon as he was born. But his ears were a problem. All Akita puppies are born with floppy ears, but Homan's were floppier than most. "The ears are the hardest thing to get right," his old friend Masutaro Ito had always said. "You want them to be erect as early as possible." Homan's ears were just hanging there. No signs of perking up.

Ito mentioned that on rare occasions a puppy's ears might not lift for several months. This gave Morie hope. "At the very least," Ito said, "a puppy's ears should begin to show signs of becoming more erect, or at least lifting, by twelve weeks." But at twelve weeks old, Homan's ears were still down. At fourteen weeks, when Ito said the ears needed to be definitely on their way to rising, Homan's still weren't doing anything.

Morie tried taping Homan's ears onto flat popsicle sticks, but Homan scratched off the sticks and ate them. Then Morie made rice glue and sculpted it onto the backs of Homan's ears in an effort to train them to grow straight upward, but Homan hated the glue and rubbed his head against the fence until the glue flaked off. Finally, at six months old—when Morie was about to give up—Homan's ears suddenly lifted, but even so, they looked a little wide and wobbly on the sides, like a bat's.

Still convinced that within Homan there was magic yet to be revealed, and hidden bits of Three Good Lucks waiting to emerge, Morie decided to use him as his stud dog. 1953. 1954. 1955. Year after year, generation after generation of puppies came from Homan. 1956. 1957. For Morie, there was nothing so exciting as watching a birth. "I always worried so much—and was full of expectations," he says. "You're not supposed to touch the puppies until the mother has a chance to lick them, but sometimes I couldn't help myself. I wanted to pick them up so badly—and couldn't wait."

He carefully inspected and weighed them, and eventually bathed them, clipped and groomed and weaned and fed and exercised them—and fussed over them with great hope. He examined their poop, smelled their breath. And he began training them with a loud voice—and loud praise—and never raised a hand.

When it was time to decide which puppy to keep—and which to give away—Morie became frustrated and irritable. It was such a hard decision, and he was always difficult to live with as he contemplated the possibilities, and considered what he was looking for in the next dog. Even at six or eight weeks old, the puppies were almost impossible to separate into categories of good and not-so-good dogs.

Studying his notes, and the dog wisdom he had absorbed over the years, Morie tried to make a science of it, creating a list of qualities that he was looking for in an Akita as a way to establish a method of selection.

A puppy needed to have a good thick coat, to start with. This was essential in a snow country dog. Next, you had to pay attention to the shape of the head. The Akita's head was surely one of the most distinctive features of the breed but sometimes it didn't reach mature form until the dog was three or four years old. Morie found if he looked closely, there were signals early on. You could see signs of cheekiness and a broad head in a puppy. A wide head is what you wanted, and in those years, a broad muzzle. And the dog's profile needed to show a distinct stop, which is the drop from the forehead to the muzzle.

A puppy's eye shape didn't change very much as it matured. If the eyes were round on a puppy, they would stay that way—and never become the desired triangular shape. A puppy's tail should be set high and curling up over the back—right away. Eventually, Morie observed that the size of the bumps on a puppy's legs—right above the paw—indicated how large and tall he'd become when full grown.

A puppy's temperament was the simplest thing to judge. Morie

A bump above the paw told Morie
how tall the dog would be

had made some mistakes in the past, but usually a dog's personality was fairly obvious if you observed littermates playing. You could study how aggressively a puppy competed for food and territory, and which dogs were naturally bolder. As soon as the puppies were weaned, Kitako fed them and came to know them well—and always had great sweeping pronouncements about which dogs were superior and which ones Morie should consider keeping. She always fell for the sweet ones, and the docile, people-oriented puppies, and she made the mistake of giving them names, too, which only made it harder to see them go. The children liked the reckless puppies with spunk, or the runts that trailed after them hoping for affection.

As for Morie, he watched the puppies wrestling each other in their pen or romping in the garden and looked for signs of greatness, for hints of something brave and noble and loyal. He looked for things that reminded him of Three Good Lucks—a feeling of balance and poise, perspective and intelligence, authority and awareness. He also looked for things that reminded him of other ancestor dogs that he knew of, echoes of an aunt or great aunt, a grandfather. Things that had been passed down. "I always wanted to breed confident dogs," he says. He looked for energy and endurance, a ruggedness and competitive spirit. *"I'm not trying to breed pets,"* he used to say to Kitako when she made her preferences known. There was a difference between a loyal dog and a merely affectionate one. There was a difference between ruggedness and playfulness. Morie hoped that one day he might raise a dog that could save somebody's life.

Even with his lists and notes and observations, Morie was confounded time and time again. He'd pick a puppy—thinking it was just what he wanted—and then watch it grow up to disappoint him as it matured. Other times, he was frustrated to see a dog that he'd given away become incredibly beautiful and strong. Puppies grew in

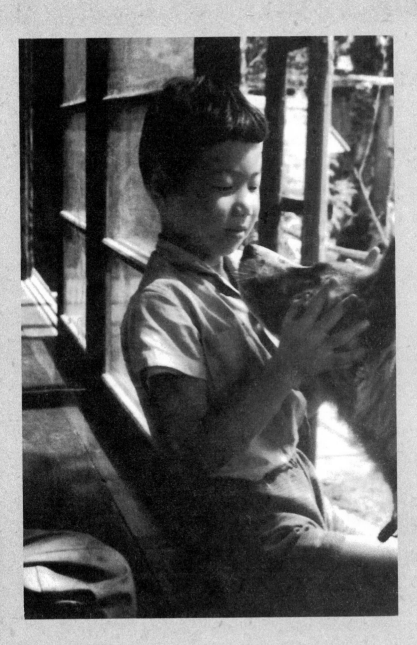

Mamoru and the other children loved needy dogs

spurts, and quickly, and could look ungainly until they were two years old. Occasionally the most pathetic puppy became a champion or an ugly dog, like Kurosawa-Tora, had heroic qualities.

A few times, when Kitako was strongly attached to a dog that he didn't really care for, Morie kept it for her—but never told her why. But most of the time, he held his ground. "We've had many dis-agreements about puppies," he says. "And it was hard. But I wanted a dog with a strong will, a vigorous dog with *kishō*. It may be a bit rough. It's not a dog for the house. Kitako tends to fall for the sweet dogs. If we were lucky, we'd get a dog that was both."

New puppies were a magnet for visitors and a cause for cele-bration. When one of Morie's dogs had a litter, all the dog buddies and aspiring breeders appeared at the house, lingering around the puppy pen. The dogs were carefully examined and preferences were expressed, usually after a great deal of sake. The dog crowd was always looking for puppies in exchange for favors or future stud fees, and their conversation always gravitated to wheeling and deal-ing. Kitako urged Morie to sell the puppies and charge stud fees out-right. They were beautiful dogs, greatly admired and worth so much money. She hated to see them handed out foolishly after a night of drinking. Morie just ignored her, or sat quietly and waited for her tirade to end. He didn't want to get rich or make money with the puppies. More than anything, he wanted to do something good with them. When he heard that an acquaintance, Gentaro Ishii, had lost all his possessions in a house fire—and then all his savings at the horse races—Morie gave him four puppies from one of Homan's lit-ters, hoping he'd sell them and buy a new house.

Homan sired lots of puppies in those years and Kitako often felt frustrated in trying to find original names for them. There was

Hachiman I, Hachiman II, and then Hachiman III. Hachiman was the name of an ancient Shinto deity who was venerated in several large shrines in the area, and said to protect warriors and a community in general.

Morie loved the Hachimans and believed in them, but he couldn't help but notice that their ears were wobbly and difficult—the rice glue didn't always work—and their skin was getting looser with each generation. Three Good Lucks had a coat as thick and tight as Goromaru's, and Morie had been careful to breed Homan and the Hachimans to bitches that were equally thick-coated and taut-looking, but somehow, in spite of his efforts, the coat on each generation of dogs seemed to get softer and thinner. "The Goromaru thickness was fading away," Morie says. With each generation the dogs were losing their vigor and getting smaller, too. Eventually Morie concluded that they were reversal dogs, inside and out, the whole lot of them.

There had been too much inbreeding within a small gene pool, and the recessive traits that had been silent and hidden inside Three Good Lucks were linking up with a set of similarly silent recessive traits—and becoming predominant. "I wondered where to go with my breeding," Morie says. "I had all these fine Goromaru descendants, but they seemed to need an extra boost of something."

It wasn't just Morie's dogs, though. Looking around at the litters of puppies being born all over the snow country by the mid-1950s, Morie concluded that Akitas everywhere were suffering from inbreeding. The Goromaru descendants had a tendency to get a soft coat and lose their shape. Kongo descendants had loose skin, wrinkles around the face, and their tails barely curled at all. The coat became much blacker, too dark. They seemed to be getting thinner, too.

"Once your dogs start going in the wrong direction," Morie says, "it's hard to turn things around. It can take ten years to get things back on course. Color might be great, but ears are strange. And once the ears start being a problem, it's serious."

Breeding a great Akita—or even an average, healthy, decent dog—seemed increasingly to Morie like a difficult, often heartbreaking undertaking. He had come to feel about dogs as he did about judo, or engineering, or gardening, or building, or almost anything else he loved in life. Things that were worth mastering took time and patience. With dogs, you could sometimes fool yourself that you knew what you were doing, but you didn't.

When Morie tried to talk about these things at an Akita Preservation Society meeting, he found himself outnumbered by new breeders—all businessmen who'd jumped on the Akita bandwagon to get rich. The notion of the breed, and where it was heading, seemed of little interest to them. "Money was all they talked about," Morie says. Disillusioned, he returned home and wondered aloud to his friends and family whether he should quit judging and drop off the board of the Preservation Society. Increasingly he felt like an outsider, the one who cared more about dogs than hype. Masutaro Ito urged him to stay on. And surprisingly, so did Kitako. "Don't give up," she said. "It's important to you."

The dog world had changed. Morie worried that he might wind up changing with it. He missed the old snow country perspective, the feeling of patience and balance. He missed the innocence too. There was something about the mix of dogs and money that had never sat well with him. For years he'd been coming up with excuses for not selling his puppies and, at the same time, making lists in his head of people to whom he'd like to give them away. Nothing felt as rewarding—as lastingly good—as giving a puppy away. Just to see the expression on a friend's face. They'd hold the puppy and look at Morie like they couldn't believe their luck. In what other ways in life can you offer somebody a gift like that, or make them feel as good? It was in the years of the reversal dogs, amid the crazy greed and herd thinking, that Morie finally made up his mind: He would never sell a dog for money, no matter what.

Atsuko and One Hundred Tigers

Five

The Dog Who Lost His Tail in the Fence

White dogs were unpopular for a period of ten or twelve years after the war. Of course it was ridiculous, but everybody in the snow country went along. Nobody was interested in breeding white dogs, or showing them. Morie was always curious about how a dog trend like that got started. He guessed the bias against white dogs began during the war, when the Japanese military refused to buy white fur pelts. White was a color associated with death and worn at Shinto funerals, so there might have been a superstition that lining a military coat in white fur was bad luck.

The funny thing was, lots of old snow country legends portrayed white dogs as magical spirits or spiritual rescuers. And in ink drawings and paintings done by Zen monks centuries ago, a white dog was often a representation of Buddha, an expression of pure goodness and compassion. But somehow those traditions had been forgotten—or people didn't care anymore.

Always a contrarian, Morie took a squirmy white puppy from a dog buddy who didn't want it. The dog had a strong neck and curling tail and big sweet black eyes. Kitako named him One Hundred Tigers because he wasn't a typically serene and catlike Akita. He was high-spirited and curious and liked to wander. The children loved him, especially Mamoru, who was always running after him.

In the spring of 1957, Morie registered One Hundred Tigers in a big show and, to the dog crowd's astonishment, he won first prize. Morie was counting on more victories in the ring until the white dog returned one day from an off-leash excursion in the mountains with his tail hanging limp. He'd cut himself somehow—gotten caught in barbed wire or on the sharp splinter of a fallen tree. Morie took him to soak in the hot springs, where the water contained sulfur and other minerals, and then he made a mineral-mud plaster for the dog's wound and let it dry. But two weeks later when Morie came out to feed the dogs, One Hundred Tigers was romping around in one corner of his kennel and his white tail was lying still in another. The dog had rubbed his tail against the fencing and it had fallen off.

He was still a good dog, "but I couldn't show an Akita without a tail," Morie says. "He would have been disqualified, and worse, everybody would laugh. A good dog doesn't like being laughed at."

DURING THE WAR, Morie had to be resourceful and creative to get a power plant built and running, often coming up with his own solutions to engineering problems. But now that his company was flush with cash and determined to use the latest technology, problem-solving had changed. Money was spent freely. When Morie encountered a snag at a plant, suddenly a dozen engineers arrived from Tokyo to examine the site and offer solutions that were decided by committee. "During the war, I really had to use my brain," Morie says. "Afterwards, it was almost too easy."

Japan was rushing to become as modern as possible, as quickly as possible, and Morie's company, which had begun as a shipping agency in the nineteenth century, developed into a vast conglomerate of semiautonomous divisions: breweries, chemicals, finance, mining, heavy machinery, materials, energy, real estate, technology. It made tanks and ships and buses before and during the war, as well as beer, glass, paper, and electrical appliances. Most of these divisions were forced to disband after the war, or were spun off into independent enterprises. But in the late 1950s they began regrouping under the same corporate roof. The Mitsubishi Corporation's products touched almost every part of life and its branches employed hundreds of thousands of workers who remained, in most cases, with the same company division until retirement. They drove Mitsubishi cars and drank Mitsubishi beer and cooked with Mitsubishi kitchen appliances. Their children lived in Mitsubishi-run dorms at college, and got Mitsubishi jobs when they graduated. You were a company man for life, usually—or, in a word borrowed from English, a *sararī-man*—and rather proud of that too.

サラリーマン

Sararī-man

By 1957, the company had built five power plants in Hachimantai, and one plant in Aomori. They weren't simply an enhancement of daily life in remote areas or a way for Mitsubishi to create more consumers for its electrical appliances. They were increasingly crucial to the survival of the Japanese family farm. The farmers tilled some of the most fertile and productive soil in the world, but struggled with prolonged and brutal winters, uncontrolled flooding during the snowmelt in late spring, and intermittent drought in the summer. Without electricity in many rural pockets, and without modern irrigation systems or equipment, agricultural practices hadn't changed much for centuries: Rice seedlings were planted by hand, oxen and horses pulled plows, and fields were soaked at the whim of nature.

Morie wasn't surprised to hear from Mitsubishi that three plants were scheduled to be built in the mountains of Miyagi prefecture, a bit farther south, and that he'd been selected to oversee the projects. Miyagi prefecture had its own traditions and culture—its own distinct regional character—and it wasn't a dog-crazy place like Akita. In fact, there weren't many dogs in Miyagi at all, and considering the frenzy of dog breeding in the north, that might be a relief. In any case, Morie welcomed change and figured he'd make do. The company had found a house for him, not far from the Hanayama Dam. Morie was told the house was perfectly nice—the finest house in the area—but, regrettably, it didn't compare to the spacious country estate he'd been enjoying in Hachimantai, where he had built barns, kennels, chicken coops, guest rooms, three ponds, a vegetable garden, grape arbors, fruit orchards, and created a system of indoor plumbing and hot water delivery. As a reward for his hard work—and in consideration of his industriousness—Morie was told that he could keep the Hachimantai house for as long as he wished. The company thought he might want to use it as a weekend retreat or summer house. He had made so many improvements to the property, it seemed only fair.

"Where will the new power plant president and his family live in Hachimantai?" Morie asked his superiors. The man who would be succeeding him was a dedicated executive and Morie was certain there wasn't another house nice enough for him. It didn't seem right for Morie to keep a big place for his family to use only on weekends, or in the summer, while his hardworking colleague had to survive every day in a house less grand and less comfortable. After consulting with Kitako, Morie turned down the company's offer. "I wanted the new plant president to have the house in Hachimantai," Morie says. "It was such a nice spot. And the decision made me feel good."

With each passing year it became clearer that what made Morie feel good—more than making money or having an easy lifestyle—was a sense that he had somehow improved the world around him, left things better off, or done somebody a favor. And with each passing year, he had begun to suspect that in the great scheme of things this wasn't unequivocally true about his job building power plants. They were, like so many modern advancements that had become necessities, not attractive ones. And as much as they might have improved world commerce or industrial efficiency, there were also enormous drawbacks.

In the years since the war's end in 1945, Morie had seen country roads widened, mountains cleared, tunnels dug, valleys flooded. He'd seen Hachirogata, the massive lake near Castle No. 5 Town, the second largest in Japan, slowly siphoned off to create thousands of acres of fertile new farmland. The snow country was still largely wilderness, and sparsely populated, but thick power lines had been strung on poles along its highways. Many remote villages that for centuries had known only torches and kerosene lamps were now ablaze at night with brilliant incandescent light—something that had changed people's daily lives and routines. They worked longer, and harder. And the human energy that had been directed toward the war effort—or toward simply enduring it—was now harnessed to achieve very different, tangible goals. Morie liked that. All over the snow country, all over Japan, there was an urge to prosper, to get ahead. And Morie liked the forward movement and felt energized by the sense of progress toward a more modern life. But he couldn't help thinking about what was being lost.

Morie came up with a way to make reparations of his own. He began to plant cherry trees against one side of the power plant complex in Hachimantai. He thought it would be a nice gesture, a contribution to the landscape. But once he started planting trees, he didn't stop, and the row of trees became a stand of trees and then a grove. He got friends to donate trees, or transplant them. He padded his operating budget and bought more. Eventually, Morie's cherry trees formed a circle around the Hachimantai plant, swept up the slope of the mountain, and in the spring, clouds of pink blossoms covered the hillside. Before leaving Akita and Aomori prefectures to move south, Morie planted cherry trees at all the facilities under his management, and later on, in Hanayama and Kurikoma too. They became his signature, almost an apology of sorts: Wherever Morie had built a power plant, there would also be cherry trees. One thousand in all.

KITAKO'S REACTION TO the news of moving south to the Hanayama area was immediately positive—almost jubilant—because it brought her closer to civilization. Looking on a map of Miyagi prefecture, she was thrilled to see that Kamaguchi, the village where they would be living, wasn't too far from Sendai, the prefecture's largest city. Kitako imagined shopping trips to Sendai, and finding good wool cardigans and crisp white cotton blouses, and better shoes, as well as feasting on the city's cultural events and other offerings. She imagined introducing her children to city life and better schools for Atsuko and Ryoko. There was an excellent private high school in Sendai and Moritake was already twelve—ready to begin soon. And though Sendai had been heavily bombed during the war, it was quickly being rebuilt and replanted. Promotional campaigns called it "The City of Trees," for Sendai's commitment to the restoration of its famous green and parklike setting.

But, even better, Kitako would now be closer to Tokyo—and to her family, particularly the two sisters to whom she'd remained close. Her sister Mitsuko was married to an executive at Isuzu, a company that made cars and heavy equipment. Kitako's brother-in-law, Soichi Otomo, was head of the materials division and a serious man with a serious job that brought him an impressive salary and a busy social life with Mitsuko. While living in Hachimantai, Kitako only saw her sister once a year, when Mitsuko brought her children up north to spend the summer in the mountains with their cousins. The Otomo children, Yoko and Susumu, were close in age to Kitako's—and had grown close to them over the years.

On those visits, Mitsuko would arrive at the train station claiming to be exhausted by the long ride but looking so fresh in her beautiful city suits and heels. She was thin and delicate and, unlike Kitako's, her hands were soft and showed no signs of housework. She always brought perfectly wrapped boxes of specialty foods from Tokyo and usually gifts of clothing for Kitako—stylish things of good quality that she knew were difficult for her sister to find in the countryside. "My sisters always sent nice things, or brought me clothes," Kitako says. "Nobody wanted me to look like a mountain lady."

Each summer, as she received her sister and her gifts, Kitako felt grateful but self-conscious, wondering what Mitsuko must think of her modest circumstances. In the world where she and her sisters were raised—a world that had burned to ash during the war and was now miraculously reviving—if you married a man from the country, as Kitako had, you were supposed to marry a man with an estate and farmland and lots of servants to help you. You weren't supposed to wind up scrubbing floors yourself, doing laundry by hand, cooking over a woodstove, or feeding a bunch of hungry dogs in your spare moments.

Every summer, after Mitsuko's arrival, the sisters would stay up late talking after dinner. Kitako had always been a realist and didn't believe in pretending everything was fine, but at the same time, what was the point of burdening her sister with complaints? Each passing year there was less to say. Their lives were increasingly so different. Mitsuko had begun working as an executive secretary in the office of National Cash Register, an American company, and seemed more sophisticated and busier than ever. She never stayed in the mountains for long. After spending one night, she got back on the train for Tokyo in the morning, leaving her two children behind with Kitako for five or six weeks. She knew they'd have a good time—the outdoors and fresh air was so healthy for kids—but Mitsuko never cared for the snow country herself. Her memories of life there during the war were only bad, things she didn't care to recall or relive. Still, she always left with a tug of sadness when she said good-bye to Kitako. "We all felt sorry for her," Mitsuko says, "and how things had turned out."

There was another sister, Teruko, the oldest of the family, whom Kitako heard from occasionally. Teruko had also married well, to a Tokyo University graduate who'd gone on to great success as an executive with the Taiyo Fishery Corporation, a large fishing and fish-packing company that had almost cornered the market in whale meat, a commodity that hadn't been part of the Japanese diet to any great degree until the Americans arrived after the war and suggested it could help end the fresh meat shortages. But even before the war, Teruko and her husband, Kenji Kinoshita, had a large house in Tokyo and plenty of extra money. After the war, when the Taiyo Fishery had regrouped and revitalized itself—salmon fishing in the north, aquaculture farming, whale meat, and a large export business— things got only better. Teruko and Kenji enjoyed a swell circle of urbane friends, including several literary stars of the time (the legendary Naoya Shiga, one of the most revered novelists of modern Japan, had introduced the couple to each other), and later, a cadre of famous sports figures. Kenji's company backed a sumo grand champion, and later, the company's professional baseball team, the Yokohama Bay Stars, won the national pennant.

Baseball had been introduced in Japan in 1872, and played professionally there since 1934, but after the war, the sport mesmerized the country with its slowness and grace, and its demand for players with patience and precision and strength. By 1950, two leagues had been formed and there were dozens of pro teams—all of them owned by major corporations. Taiyo Fishery owned the Whales, and then changed their name to the Yokohama Bay Stars. In 1954, when Teruko and Kenji hosted a reception for Joe DiMaggio and Marilyn Monroe, who had come to Japan on their honeymoon, Kitako made a special visit to Tokyo. Stepping into Teruko's world for a few days was a heady experience, and one that Kitako would never forget. Teruko had a wardrobe of custom-made dresses and handmade shoes, gorgeous leather handbags, and stockings, scarves, and hats. Her friends were sophisticated and educated, chatted about recent showings of Kabuki plays, nights at the symphony, and shared opinions about Akira Kurosawa's new movie, *Shichinin no samurai* (*Seven Samurai*). The Kinoshitas had enviably glamorous lives, the kind that Kitako, after her long years in the snow country, could only vaguely imagine anymore and only occasionally wanted to. It was too painful. But now, with the prospect of trips to Sendai—and getting to Tokyo with greater frequency—things seemed much better.

But on her first trip with Morie to look over the new company house where they would be living, Kitako struggled not to fall into despair. The area around the Hanayama Dam was exquisitely beautiful and the region had many natural hot springs for bathing, but the house was much smaller—one third the size of their place in Hachimantai—and miles and miles from anything but the site of the new power plant. When she inquired about Sendai, and how long it might take to visit the city, she felt even worse. Sendai was still rubble, she was told, and "The City of Trees" was in reality a city of tiny saplings. But it was irrelevant whether Sendai had been effectively rebuilt and replanted. It was an arduous struggle to get there. Depending on the time of year, the dirt roads were either muddy or rutted or icy or simply impassable due to snow. If Kitako wanted Atsuko and Moritake to go there for a better education, they would have to become boarders at the private high school—and spend only weekends or holidays at home.

Another sad discovery was the extreme poverty of the region. While Kitako had supposed that she'd be surrounded by more modern conveniences in Miyagi prefecture, the farms around Hanayama were very backward, still without electricity, gas, or any sign of motorized farming equipment. The farmers lived in small huts and slept on hand-woven straw mats next to their horses. In winter and early spring when it was hard to find grass or hay to feed the horses, the farmers rose before dawn looking for pastures where the grass was thick and tall, and where it could be cut. "Sometimes in bad weather we'd hear the bells of their horses in the dark," says Kitako. "It was so early, they would cut grass by hand with sickles, but could hardly see a thing." The mountain snowmelt sometimes flooded the valley, sweeping away the farmers' shacks and drowning livestock. Other years brought temperatures that were simply too cold for growing good rice, and seedlings never took root. Harvest time came, but there was nothing to sell.

She'd thought the company house was too modest at first, but after moving in, Kitako realized it was a palace in comparison to any house nearby. It had wide-plank wooden floors and several rooms with tatami-mat floors, sliding shoji doors, and lovely old-fashioned cedar ceilings. Morie brought the big wooden bathtub with its electric coil from the house in Hachimantai, along with a few of his custom dog kennels. But once again Kitako found herself cooking without gas. The kitchen had a large stove that had been built with river rocks, and hanging over its open fire was a cauldron where Kitako cooked and boiled and simmered and steamed. And coughed. Ventilation was a chronic problem. "The kitchen," Mamoru remembers, "was a very smoky place."

If Kitako had a free moment to indulge in self-pity, or make a comparison between her life and the lives of her glamorous sisters in Tokyo, the world around her brought perspective. Everywhere she walked or drove the horse cart, she passed farm wives working in the fields all day. "They often had babies on their backs, the ones who were still being breast-fed," Kitako says. At the day's end, they walked home to small sheds and cabins with no heat except the fire they built themselves. Sometimes all they had to burn was dung.

Like Morie, she applauded and embraced so many of the changes Japan had made since the war. The Americans had occupied and redirected the nation for seven years—from 1945 to 1952—then left Japan to run itself. The military had been abolished. A parliamentary government had been established, leaving the imperial family to become distant celebrities. New laws protected fundamental civil liberties—the rights to free speech, a free press, and free assembly. Women had been given the right to vote. Reforms had overthrown the feudal system of land ownership, and families who had previously been tenants were given their own parcels of land to farm.

But things were still wobbly and confusing for many rural people who'd seen very little improvement in their daily lives. While the cities of Japan were being rebuilt after the devastating air raids of the war and were full of employment opportunities, many of the snow country farmers were as poor as ever. Hanayama, in particular, was miles from a train station and its isolation had really made a difference. Morie's employees at the power plant were a simple, hardworking bunch—people who'd never lived with running water in their homes, never had much education or traveled anywhere. Morie organized a bus trip to the beach for his workers and their families as soon as he learned none of them had ever seen the ocean.

Most of the plant employees had been raised on farms, but like many farmers in those days, they had been drawn away from the land to higher paying jobs that required less labor. Lots of farmers had gravitated to Sendai and Tokyo, where there seemed to be unlimited construction jobs in the effort to rebuild. Eventually these jobs became too enticing to resist—farmers began migrating to the city in the winter and spring, during the slow season, leaving their wives and children behind to run the farms in their absence. In the early summer, they'd return again for field work and the fall harvest.

"Many, many, many women and children were left alone all winter," Kitako says, "and they had so much to do, so many chores and responsibilities—keeping things going alone. If the warm weather came early, before their husbands returned, they had to plant the fields on their own. It was hard to see them so burdened."

On visits to local farms to buy staples—root vegetables, water chestnuts, miso—she was stunned by the squalor. "I felt so sorry for the children," she says. "They had runny noses and straw shoes in the winter. They ate only barley and miso-soaked vegetables for lunch." Just as often, she'd stop by a farmer's cottage and find it empty except for babies who'd been left bound inside hay bales and straw cradles. "Their mothers couldn't leave the fields to go home and change diapers," Kitako says, "so they left their babies naked in these straw cradles, tied up so they couldn't fall or squeeze out—with maybe a little extra loose straw underneath them to absorb the fluids."

Kitako would look out to the fields and see all the mothers working together, a row of white scarves over their heads, their short cotton robes and funny snow country trousers, their pale tired faces. "People always talk about how beautiful mountain women are because of their fair skin," she says, "but it's because for half the year there's no sunshine. And the other half, they're working in the fields with their heads down."

When Kitako thought about their lives, and how little they had, she found it hard not to offer to help in some way. "Theirs was such a different life than I'd ever known," she says, "and rather than detach from it, I felt that I should enter in." During an early planting season when the men were away, Kitako offered to work in the fields—and was taught how to place rice seedlings patiently, one by one, in the mud. "I did that, sitting on a short stool in the fields, with bare legs and my feet in the water." At the end of the day, she carried equipment back to the farms and noticed, to her sadness, all the farm children who'd been left at home alone "with just an old carrot to chew on, or a piece of radish."

Children as old as two were sometimes left bound to cradles during planting and harvesting season—"even children who were old enough to talk." There were no babysitters, or extra hands. Even the oldest women were expected to help in the fields. "The mothers weren't trying to be cruel. They were only concerned about keeping their children safe. But it was very hard to witness."

Realizing she had something more to offer than an extra pair of hands in the field—and inexperienced hands at that—Kitako told the farm wives that she'd be pleased to have their toddlers and older children at her house on busy farm days. She would provide snacks and lunch and they'd be free to play outside with the other children. "And once I offered, believe me, everybody came." Some days there were twenty or more children to look after, including her own. "It looked like a kindergarten," Kitako says, "except we had no toys in those days. Morie made bamboo sleds for the children in the winter, and then, in the spring, built a tree house with swings and a rope ladder where they could all play Tarzan."

Along with her new duties running an informal day care center, Kitako found herself cooking for even larger masses of people. Morie had a group of regulars, all dog buddies and big drinkers. Atsuko and Moritake also brought friends home from school and they stayed all weekend. Their village of Kawaguchi was miles from any kind of guesthouse or inn, so when Mitsubishi executives and engineers visited, there was only one place to stay and only one place to eat. "They'd come to inspect the plant or just visit to discuss improvements and overhauls," Kitako says, "and we'd have them all with us. Sometimes we'd have a dozen men from Tokyo staying with us for a month. It was hard to feed them every single meal," she says, "and just hard to be around all those men."

It was still unusual for a country woman to drive in those days—most villagers didn't own cars. But hoping for a little more freedom, Kitako decided to take driving lessons and after a few weeks, went to the next town to take a driving test. When the department of motor vehicles officer recognized her—they both had children at the same school—she was suddenly exempt from taking any kind of examination and handed a license with no charge. Amused by this, and pleased with her new license, Kitako told Morie the story as soon as she got home. "How do I know you can really drive?" he asked her. "You didn't even have to take a test!" He refused to allow her to use the car and, not long afterward, sold it.

Kitako found it impossible to stave off bitterness at times, and bouts of great anger at Morie. As his dog buddies or Mitsubishi salarymen sat around the table and drank all night, and Morie's face turned red and his voice grew louder and she heard him talking about the dogs again, sometimes Kitako would find herself fuming in the kitchen. "I should have divorced him after three weeks!" she'd say to herself. Maybe once Morie retired, things would improve. They could live in a city and enjoy more pleasant times together. But as long as she was the wife of a power plant manager, "it meant I would always live in a remote area," Kitako says. "It's like life in a lighthouse. Everything is about endurance."

In a low moment, one night after all the company men had gone to bed, she raised her voice to Morie. "When I finally die from exhaustion," she called out, "I hope the dogs will be able to take care of you."

THERE WERE THREE OR FOUR dogs at the house—One Hundred Tigers and Samurai Princess, a beautiful bitch, among them—but Morie's primary concern in those days was Hoko, a splotchy brown brindle with white paws. His coat was wonderful, as was his size, but he had a heavy, Quasimodo face with wide cheeks. Hoko's ears were slow to rise, too, and Morie fussed over them with glue and sticks and tape until they stood up on their own. Eventually, the family

Samurai Princess

gave the dog a nickname, "One Ear Floppy," which pretty much sizes up the situation. In his puppy pictures, it looks like he could have been called "Two Ears Floppy" just as well.

"He was considered a very handsome dog in 1958," explains Morie. And his ears weren't really so terrible. "It's difficult sometimes to capture the characteristics of a dog in a photograph," he says. "You can capture one thing, but not much else."

In any case, Hoko didn't stay around too long. Masutaro Ito was always looking for ways to help the villagers in Shimizu, where he was mayor. Since Ito knew a great deal about dog breeding, he came up with the idea of giving a dog to every farmer in the village as a way to increase their annual income. One litter of puppies every year might just be enough to keep a farmer going.

The only problem was, Ito's own dogs were pretty dreadful at the time. "His puppies were weak," Morie says, "and lacked *kishō*." Feeling sorry for the village of Shimizu, and thinking of all the kindness that Ito had shown him over the years, Morie eventually gave his old friend two dogs to improve his breeding stock. First, he gave him a dog named Prince the Second, who fathered a few nice litters. And then Morie handed over Hoko. "Use him well," Morie told his old friend. And Ito did. Hoko went on to win a Hall of Fame Award with Ito beside him in the ring, and then sired two Hall of Fame dogs. Ito's standing in the dog world skyrocketed, and the village of Shimizu's did too. "People came from all over to breed their dogs with Hoko's offspring," Morie says, "and the whole town was revived as a center of good dogs."

Time passed very slowly before another good dog came along, and Morie waited. Then one warm summer morning, a litter was born in the shady underside of the house and almost immediately Morie could see that one puppy had potential. He was bigger than his

Hoko and little One Hundred Tigers with the boys

littermates and had a gorgeous thick coat with spectacular coloring that faded perfectly, reminiscent of his ancestor Three Good Lucks. His tail was a knockout, curling perfectly the second he was born.

As the weeks passed, he only got better. Morie felt certain that he would become a peak dog, the finest combination of Homan and Hachiman and Three Good Lucks—and even Goromaru—possible. "I thought, Finally! I did it," Morie says. "I got it right! After so many generations!"

Very proud of this achievement, Morie decided he'd like to name the dog himself—and not leave such an important decision to Kitako. Holding the puppy in his arms one morning, he looked up to the bright sunlight, piercing and golden, and said a prayer: *Someday let this puppy shine like the morning sky.*

東 雲

Shinonome

In Japanese, this word means "dawn" or "morning light" or "daybreak," but in Morie's mind, it means "bright light from the eastern sky." And indeed, Shinonome won a national prize and garnered enormous attention, the kind of praise and ribbons that Morie had been wanting for years. The judges loved the dog. The dog crowd did too. But slowly, over time, Morie started to feel differently about him. Shinonome was aesthetically pleasing and all that, but on a deeper level something was missing.

When Morie took him into the mountains, Shinonome rarely chased a rabbit and never seemed particularly territorial. He ran slowly and was chronically incurious. The dog lacked ruggedness

Shinonome was a complacent champion

and spirit. He seemed almost too content—as if he knew he'd won the national prize and the rest of his life would be a slide downhill. Shinonome liked his kennel a little bit too much, and his bed. When Morie came out to see him, the dog barely raised his head. He seemed bored. What had caused it?

Not able to come up with an answer, Morie loaned Shinonome to the governor of Iwate prefecture. The dogs in the snowy north had endured the harshest weather on the main island of Japan for centuries. They were always feisty and spirited, but could be a little too aggressive for popular taste. Morie suspected that Shinonome's laid-back temperament might be just the right genetic antidote for them. And life in the severe cold might be just the answer for Shinonome. "Keep him as long as you want," Morie said to the governor. And he did: for the rest of Shinonome's long and extremely peaceful life.

A DOOR-TO-DOOR PEDDLER used to come by the old house in Hachimantai, a woman who sold carrots and radishes and other vegetables that were otherwise hard to find in the winter months. One morning she called out from the entrance of the house that she had some very rare herbs and roots to sell—including wild ginseng, a root that had great rejuvenating ability and was said to prolong life.

"How did you find wild ginseng?" Kitako asked her. Even before the war, when they lived in Manchuria, most of the ginseng was farm grown. Wild ginseng was almost unimaginable.

The peddler said that she had a son who lived in the mountains near Ichinoseki. He was a *matagi*, she said—an old fashioned migratory hunter—and sometimes he came across wild ginseng and other herbs and gave them to her to sell. The peddler's family name was

Uesugi, the kind of name you didn't forget. In medieval times, the Uesugi family were famous warlords who dominated the Kanto region of Japan for more than a century, but they had fallen from power in 1568. Even more unforgettable: *Matagi* were very rare in those days. You rarely met one, or even heard about them. They lived in the mountains, usually in tribes of masters and apprentices, and hunted barefoot. Legendary huntsmen, the *matagi* in Akita and Aomori prefectures were heroes of unbelievable tales, but more than anything they were a dying breed, a throwback to samurai times and well before.

As Kitako recounted the peddler's story to Morie, he recalled that he'd known a man named Uesugi during the war. He was ten or fifteen years older than Morie—and an unforgettable figure, a charmer who helped the farmers in Ichinoseki stay afloat by trading their rice for the highest prices on the black market in Tokyo. Uesugi was a gambler and hard drinker, really almost an outlaw. During the war, when he was smuggling rice to Tokyo for the farmers, he used to masquerade as a policeman—wearing a pristine black uniform, white gloves and black hat—to get a free seat on the train. He returned from the city with wads of cash, and white sugar, cigarettes, whiskey, and his favorite food of all: American corned beef. To the local farmers, he was a god.

Kitako and Morie had almost forgotten about the peddler's story, until one day after moving to the Hanayama area, Morie was talking to a group of villagers who told him about a licensed "inspector of the forest" who lived in Komanoyu, an old *onsen*, or hot springs spa, about twenty miles outside of town. The bathhouse roof was falling down and the place was almost uninhabitable. The forest inspector didn't mind, the villagers said. He was accustomed to much more rugged conditions. "He is a *matagi*—a real one. He has a lifetime permit to hunt year-round." The man didn't mix with regular people, they said.

"He's more comfortable with wild deer and antelope and bears." In the summer and winter, he vanished for other parts of Japan, but during the fall and spring, he served as a forest inspector and could be found patrolling the deep woods and forests between Hanayama and Kurikoma. He inspected the flora and fauna, gathered specimens, and hunted with a huge knife, a spear, and an old single-barreled shotgun.

"Is he a drinker?" Morie asked the villagers. No. He was a quiet, solitary figure. Didn't play cards or gamble, either. "Whoever this forest inspector was, I figured he couldn't possibly be Uesugi," Morie said. "The man I'd known years before drank heavily and with gusto. That wasn't likely to change."

Some months later, a tall, wiry figure suddenly appeared outside the entrance to Morie and Kitako's house. He called out, *Kombanwa!*— Good evening!—and Kitako slid open the doors. He was in his mid-fifties, but athletic and powerful looking. His hair was thick and dark and shaved down to a bristling flattop, a style that had been popular six or seven decades earlier. His small mustache was unusual too, almost as dated as the carefully shaped ponytail of the samurai. And tucked into the collar of his heavy overcoat, he wore a colorful silk scarf.

"Is this the house of Sawataishi?" he asked. Years before, he'd known a fine man with that name.

His voice was deep and resonant, and there was something fiercely intense about him, the way he stood so erect and still and stared so intently at Kitako. He seemed utterly calm and relaxed but charged the air around him at the same time. He had a narrow gap between his front teeth, Kitako noticed, but still, it managed to become part of a wonderful smile. He introduced himself as Uesugi and bowed very deeply.

Kitako asked him to please come inside. Her husband would be home soon. Uesugi removed his *zori*—it was late autumn, already quite cold, and it was strange to see a person wearing only sandals and thin cotton *tabi* or socks, at a time when everybody else wore heavy boots. Uesugi's coat was different too, long and old-fashioned and lined with some kind of soft brown fur. He pulled off several fabric pouches that he'd been carrying, and set them down. Kitako wondered if there were knives in the pouches, or guns. Or perhaps something dead?

He was a true mountain man—almost wild. But at the same time, Kitako felt a connection with him, and a funny kind of gratitude: He bowed so deeply, and looked at her with such solemn respect, a reverence and attention, that was rare to see in a man from the snow country. "And I also thought," Kitako says, "I'd never seen anybody so handsome in my life."

Uesugi came by quite often that autumn, until the deep winter snows in December drove him away, farther south. He traveled all the way to Osaka then, on foot, in his *tabi* and snowshoes, migrating from snowy forest to snowy forest, sleeping in abandoned bear caves and beside fallen trees. His clothing grew heavier and more eccentric: fox pelts around his neck, wool scarves wrapping his head, a wide-brimmed hat with rabbit fur earflaps. He carried a shotgun inside his coat, a knife at his waist, and a fishing hook and line curled in a pocket. And in the fabric pouches that he slung over his shoulders, he kept dry rice, miso, toasted green tea, shavings of ginseng, and chunks of *kumanoi*—the dried gall bladder of a Moon Bear.

Traveling south, he visited the children he'd had with various women who might have been wives, or not wives, but with whom he had made binding domestic arrangements. Aside from them, the only house he'd visit, or sleep in, was Morie and Kitako's. Every fall and spring he came. They never knew when he'd arrive, only how: after dinner, often very late. The dogs would bark. A minute later, his deep voice would call out *Kombanwa*, and Uesugi would be standing under the lamplight.

Six

Victory Princess

Victory Princess was dumped on Morie. She was barking and harassing patients outside a new private hospital in Masaka, the next village over. She'd been mistreated or neglected somehow— her fur was encrusted with dirt and excrement—and she snapped if anybody tried to touch her. She was a brown dog, maybe a year old, and since she was shaped like an Akita, Dr. Sato, who owned the hospital, told his X-ray technician, a dog lover, to take her to Morie's.

She growled and snarled when Morie gave her a bath. "Hey!" he said, holding her firmly at the back of the neck. He rubbed the bar of soap into her wet fur and rinsed her with a pail of clear warm water—and her color changed. With each soap and rinse, she grew lighter and lighter, going from dark brown to beige to the color of a cloud, the color of snow. As Morie began to towel her off, he realized she was the most glorious white dog he'd ever seen.

But so nasty! She growled and snapped in the air—and bit Morie, or at least tried. "But at the same time," Morie says, "I could see she was a nice dog. She was sensitive and full of spirit. These are rare and important things. And I knew that Dr. Sato was counting on me to know what to do."

As it turns out, Morie did. "It wasn't so difficult really," he says. "As long as a dog bites, I don't feed it. You have to be determined, that's all. The dog's hungry and it gets frustrated. She might start growling for food on the second or third day, but of course, I still don't feed it—not if she's growling. I hear a growl and I feed the dog nothing. *Nothing.* Believe me, you aren't killing the dog. You are saving it, creating a dog that can live with people and not get shot.

"After about four or five days—it has never taken longer than that—the dog will stop growling when I approach the kennel. She realizes that aggression isn't getting her anywhere. If I approach and the dog wags her tail, then I let her lick on a bone or a small piece of food. If she wags her tail again, she gets more licks of the bone or another tiny piece of food. When she jumps up and wags her tail to see me, that's when I feed her. Every time she jumps and wags, I feed her more.

"After going through this period of difficult training, Victory Princess became loyal and devoted, even more protective of me than the other dogs," Morie says. "Actually, this is true of all of my most difficult dogs. If a dog has a behavior problem or is more difficult, I wind up having a closer relationship with it. We have a special bond that I don't have with the others. They become really cute, actually, and sensitive. Victory became very sweet, too, and one of Kitako's favorites. And after many litters, she gave us Happiness, one of the great dogs of all time."

. . .

By 1964 KITAKO HAD an electric rice cooker, a propane grill for cooking breakfast mackerel, and an electric heater that she fired up under the low dining room table when entertaining special guests on cold winter days, a Japanese tradition called *kotatsu*. The first black-and-white television arrived in September 1964—a special offer from Mitsubishi—but there was constant disagreement about where to put the thing and what to watch. Not long afterward, a big white refrigerator was delivered to the kitchen, out of the blue, and Kitako thought it was another generous company gift until she noticed the payment being deducted from Morie's salary each month.

The television came just in time for the opening ceremonies of the summer Olympic games of 1964. They were held that year in Tokyo, the first city in Asia to host them, and had been a much discussed topic at Morie and Kitako's. Kitako's family house in Azabu—rebuilt after the war and occupied by two of Kitako's younger sisters—had been purchased by a developer for the construction of a fabulous new high-rise. Along with thousands of their old Tokyo neighbors, the sisters had relocated to the city's outskirts where the real estate was more affordable. Kitako missed having an excuse to see Azabu, even though most of the familiar sites of her hometown had vanished long ago. The city landscape teemed with *gaijin*—foreigners—and glistened with new high-rise apartment buildings, new highways, new subways, new trains and cars. Kitako had mixed feelings about all of it. Along with the sadness that change brings, she felt pride too. If there were a worldwide competition for speed and sophistication, Japan seemed to be gaining ground. Not far from her old neighborhood, the fastest trains in the world, *Shinkansen* bullet trains, were running between Tokyo and the south, traveling so quickly they seemed to have pulled the wondrous future even closer.

The sense of optimism within Japan was infectious in those days, Kitako had noticed. The excitement over the Olympics had even made its way up north to the quiet towns and villages of the snow country, where thousands of new television sets were tuned to the swimming and gymnastics events, the volleyball and judo, as well as a special exhibition of sumo wrestling.

Morie wasn't really sure about Western sports, like tennis. The action kept moving, everything happened too quickly, and there wasn't enough time for breaks, for a moment to drink and talk. He didn't like the feeling of not knowing the rules of these games and being so uninformed. Sumo wrestling was so much better. The fights only lasted a few seconds, and left plenty of time for placing bets and talking, or rehashing the previous match. Friends came to the house to watch, and friends of friends, and neighbors, and kids—Atsuko came home from college with a boyfriend, Noritsugu Fukushima, a cheerful guy with a dry wit, whom everybody loved—and Morie kept picking up the television and hauling it to a bigger room. But when the entire house got hooked on women's volleyball—Japan's team was undefeated—cheering and screaming during the games, and then crying at the final match when the women beat the Russians and stepped onto the platform to receive their gold medals, Morie kept disappearing into another room to read his Akita club newsletters or wandering off to sit with the dogs. He disliked the noise, and the cheering, even the excitement. Watching tiny images of women jumping and hitting a ball over a net seemed like a waste of time.

Sometimes he started up his motorbike and took a ride. He didn't keep a car in those days, but had two motorbikes that he loved—a small one for quick trips in good weather, a larger one for heavy loads and winter. He rode them to the power plant, into town for provisions, into Akita City for meetings, and even down into Sendai, where Ryoko and Moritake were in school. For the semiannual dog shows in Odate, he borrowed a friend's truck or went with Wataru Ito, the X-ray technician from Dr. Sato's hospital who worked on the side as a dog handler.

On the way home from the big dog show, Morie sometimes stopped by Castle No. 5 Town to see the places of his childhood. He'd visit the spot where the old wooden house of his ancestors had been torn down to make way for a neighborhood development of stucco houses with metal roofs. He'd climb the hill to the shrine and the castle and marvel again at how the view had changed. The massive lake where he'd sailed as a boy had been drained to create farmland so fertile that the first year it was cultivated, the price of rice had temporarily crashed due to oversupply.

Usually on trips to Castle No. 5 Town he dropped by his sister's house to pay a visit. Haru was married with two children and on a Dale Carnegie kick in those days. She carried a copy of *How to Win Friends and Influence People* wherever she went—"just looking at the book made me feel good," she says. Inspired by the positive can-do American philosophy, she had started her own door-to-door kimono business. She began with just a few ideas and a few fabrics, but in a short time was buying up real estate in Castle No. 5 Town. "Traditionally, a kimono seller would come to the back door, the way a servant or salesman would," Haru says. "And when she was selling, she wouldn't wear a nice kimono herself. But I read Carnegie's book and he said if you want to sell things, look good, walk in the front door, and arrive as an equal—not a salesperson. So I tried that. I got dressed up in a beautiful kimono as though I were making a social call. I went to the front door. And I started selling so many kimonos that way, you couldn't believe it. Everybody wanted to look as good as I did!"

Haru had a strong presence and personality. She wore makeup like a geisha, and liked to talk about her accomplishments. She was the embodiment of another Carnegie book that she loved, *How to Stop Worrying and Start Living*. But when Morie visited her, he never asked about her kimono business or anything about Dale Carnegie. He wasn't completely sure he liked the idea of his sister working, but probably more than that, he just wasn't interested in business, or whatever it was that Haru had done to become so prosperous. "Everybody knew if you wanted to get Morie-san in a good mood, or talking at all," Haru says, "it was about dogs or nothing."

The truth is, the more modern and driven and noisy the world became, the quieter Morie got. From his sister's perspective, he hadn't changed very much. "He was always lost in a crowd," she says. "My parents had ten children—five boys followed by five girls—and he was right in the middle. Number five, the youngest boy. Nobody paid much attention to him. He wandered off and learned to fend for himself. And I think he became strong from the lack of attention and focus."

Morie liked being in the mountains. It wasn't that he resisted change, or hated modern life. It wasn't as if he didn't believe in faster cars or better refrigerators or televisions, or machines that washed your clothes and then dried them. He'd helped to electrify the snow country, after all. And he'd quite enjoyed the hubbub of the Olympics, particularly the sumo. But in the years when all of Japan seemed to be learning to eat hamburgers and play tennis and win friends and stop worrying, and all the kids, like young Mamoru, were lingering indoors in their dark bedrooms and listening to Beatles records from dawn to dusk, or sitting motionless in front of new television sets, Morie was spending more time outdoors than ever. He'd be gone for days sometimes. He slept in snow dens and built fires in caves. He pole-vaulted across creeks and ponds with tree branches. He studied the differences between poisonous wild mushrooms and the edible varieties ("it took me many years to feel confident when I ate one"). He tracked rabbits and deer and learned to catch fish using the maggots inside the bark of a beech tree for bait.

Everybody else had gotten faster and busier. Morie had gotten slower and more single-minded. And while modern life seemed more complicated but more convenient, Morie had gravitated to the essential and the difficult: He craved the natural world, the mysteries of its woods and groves and meadows, the primal focus of the hunt, and the company of dogs.

His life was changing as much as anybody's had, but seemed to have gone in the reverse direction. In the four years since Uesugi, the barefoot hunter, had first stopped by the house, he'd been a powerful catalyst. Every spring and fall when he was living in the mountains nearby, he returned frequently to see Morie and Kitako. And as much as Dale Carnegie had changed Haru or General MacArthur had changed Japan, Morie had been altered by the *matagi*.

YEARS LATER, KITAKO would say how fantastic he was with children—affectionate and attentive—but in the days when she still had young kids and teenagers at home, she kept them away from Uesugi. It was the shotgun. Late at night, when Uesugi sat down to drink and talk with Morie and Kitako, he brought the gun into the room, swaddled in fabric, and set it down on the table behind him.

Sometimes the children would wake and hear Uesugi's voice in the middle of the night. He was as loud as Morie and told funny stories that really got Kitako laughing. For a man who spent most of his days alone in the woods and mountains, he managed to know all the village news and was avidly amused by human behavior. He took note of subtle things that people did, small gestures, details that would have gone unnoticed by others.

Kitako was always leaving for the kitchen and returning to the tatami room with another tray of food—bite-size things, small bowls of mountain vegetables, marinated pork, squid, bean curd, or fresh sashimi from a morning's trip to a nearby pond where the proprietor caught and wrapped the fresh carp for her. She would pour beer for the men and sit at the low table with them. Uesugi always remembered to pour for her, keeping her small glass full. She'd been surprised to notice, on his first visit, that he had good table manners—the best manners of anyone—and held his chopsticks well, high-style, in an old formal way.

He always arrived with delicacies to share, things he'd produce from pockets of his coat or pouches around his neck. He came with sake or salmon. He brought wild berries or fresh meat—Ezo deer, antelope, rabbit—or *kumanoi*, the gall bladder of the last black bear he'd encountered. *Matagi* were trained as bear hunters, and it was part of Uesugi's job as forest inspector to keep the bear population under control. They menaced the villages in those days, and attacked children and livestock. Occasionally he'd come across a Moon Bear, a black bear with a white crescent on its chest; its *kumanoi* was so prized in China and Korea as medicine that could cure anything, it sold for more than its weight in gold.

"My *kumanoi* is the best," Uesugi would boast, and pull out his mountain knife and slice thin pieces of the black coal-like substance and then drop shavings into a cup of green tea or a pot that Kitako was brewing. While Kitako would pour, Uesugi would say, "Look at the way my *kumanoi* sinks in that cup! See how it swirls in circles at the bottom! That's how you know it's the real thing."

Sometimes the children hid behind the sliding doors of the tatami room and eavesdropped on the conversation or stared at the *matagi*'s strange clothes in the entrance—his old-style coat with its soft lining of fur, the odd pelts and scarves, the handmade snowshoes he left dripping on the stone floor. Uesugi was legendary all over the region, in the villages of Kawaguchi and Ichinoseki and Kurikoma where he traded *kumanoi* and bear meat for provisions and sake, or gambled his earnings in all-night card games—he played the *hanafuda*, or flower cards. The village kids called him "Uncle Mustache," but the men who shot dice or played cards with Uesugi had another nickname for him: *Naniwa no tatsu*. Dragon of Osaka.

Mamoru still remembers the sound of Uesugi's heavy footfall—his peculiar duck-footed gait—as he walked down the hall to the bathroom at night. The *matagi* still lived at the dilapidated *onsen* up in the hills where he could soak in the natural hot springs anytime, but he marveled at Morie's old fire-heated tub and often accepted the invitation to use it. Inside the house, he always wore the same thing: snow country trousers, a long-sleeved shirt, a cotton kimono top tied with a rope belt. Most unusual, though, was the way he always wrapped his neck with a colorful scarf.

When Mamoru was a teenager, he learned the reason for the scarf. Once, he saw Uesugi right after a bath and the *matagi*'s upper body was covered entirely in tattoos—from the top of his neck to his waist, an interlocking pattern of ancient designs "like something you'd see on a savage," Mamoru says. In Japan, tattoos were worn only by rough firemen or *Yakuza* gangsters. Even a small tattoo meant you weren't a respectable person or, at least, you weren't a person who cared to be considered respectable. Years later Uesugi told Mamoru that he thought his tattoos were beautiful and that they looked particularly good after a bath. He liked to soak in the hot water, drink sake, and then open a window to let the frigid mountain air in the steamy room. "My skin changes color then," he told Mamoru, "and my tattoos become incredible."

Uesugi was never interested in television or listening to the radio. He never used the phone. He just liked to drink and talk. When he was alone with Kitako, he always asked her how things were going—how the house was running, how the money was holding up, and how the kids were doing. Bright and disciplined, Atsuko had gotten a scholarship to study at a teachers college near Mount Fuji after turning down her uncle Kinoshita's offer to arrange a marriage for her to a professional baseball player. (Morie had hoped she'd accept the offer.) And in 1963, after quite a bit of finagling and resourcefulness, Kitako had scraped together enough money to send Ryoko—the smartest of the bunch—to veterinary school.

Kitako complained to Uesugi that her husband seemed uninterested in the careers of his daughters. He refused to talk about sending them to university until Moritake, their eldest son, had failed his college entrance exams. Saddled with the responsibility of managing the family finances, Kitako expressed frustration that Morie still refused to accept money for his puppies, when selling just one good dog might cover college tuition for both girls. Uesugi offered to intervene—and afterward did so on many occasions. He found a way to take Kitako's side gently, without creating more resistance. ("Morie-san," he'd say in a joking voice, "you should be more careful and stop spending all your money on the dogs.") And no matter how much he drank, he had a way of remaining "untouched by it,"

Kitako says, and no matter how late he stayed, Uesugi never wanted any kind of futon or regular bed. He sat upright in a chair until he fell asleep there.

MORIE WAS INCREDIBLY FLATTERED the first time Uesugi asked him to go hunting, not long after they'd met, maybe in the late fall of 1961. So excited, Morie had trouble sleeping the night before, and imagined dark caves, and wild bears roaring and barking. But in the early morning, as they drank tea and watched the orange sun rise, Uesugi suggested that they go out for pheasant. It was late autumn and cold already. The snow had come early. "This is a good time for pheasant broth with soba noodles," Uesugi said. The two men talked about the broth briefly, and how delicious it was, while they walked with Victory Princess for a couple miles to the dam. "Bring Victory," Uesugi had said. He seemed very curious about whether such a beautiful dog could hunt. Morie suspected that he himself might be under examination too.

Stopping at a quiet corner near the dam, Uesugi showed Morie the spot where he liked to wait for the birds, near their roosting place in the trees. The two men crouched in their snowshoes and tried to be as silent as possible. Morie wore a heavy wool coat lined with quilted flannel. Uesugi, wearing so many layers of dangling scarves and pelts, looked like a samurai hippie. He had a special armband too, a tattered purple and blue piece of cloth that he wore over the left sleeve of his old coat, a permit from the national park service to hunt year-round wherever he pleased. Victory sat near Morie, and before the men had heard anything, the dog stood up and stared intently at the shrubs.

Uesugi looked at the dog, and nodded approvingly at Morie.

DOG MAN

The wild pheasants ran out into the clearing, with flutters and weird sounds, a metallic whirring sound that echoed across the water. Their heads looked too big, and their tails incredibly long and splendid. Morie had thought pheasants only ran around, kind of crazily, and rarely flew, but one of them rose over his head. Victory stood still, and so did Morie, as Uesugi lifted the nose of his long single-barreled shotgun and fired. A bird fell from the sky. "If you can't kill something with one shot," Uesugi had said when they walked, "you don't deserve to kill it at all." He brought the gun down, reloaded, and waited. When another pheasant appeared, he fired again.

Morie had learned to shoot in China, in the Sino-Japanese War, and when it was his turn, he raised the double-barreled gun and brought down two birds, one after another. The feeling of the gun's vibration and the deafening sound took him back to the war, to the bombs and cacophonous explosions, the heightened feeling of being more alive than ever. It was cold in the snow, sitting there. Uesugi didn't speak for a long time. There were more birds coming, and more to shoot. The morning was tense but wonderful, and also nerve-wracking. When Uesugi finally stood up to leave, it was clear that Morie had done all right, Victory too, even though it was hard to get her to bring back the dead birds at first. She wanted to hoard them for herself.

Kitako squealed in excitement when the men returned to the house with a bag of pheasants, and she immediately drew Uesugi into a discussion about how to properly pluck and prepare the birds. It was better if you let the birds dry out first—if you hung their carcasses outside for a few days—but Kitako was eager to try some broth right away.

Morie started to feel queasy. And the thought of pheasant broth, no matter how excellent a cook Kitako was, disgusted him. He didn't want to think about the flesh of the birds boiling and simmering, or the skin of the bird becoming rubbery, or the bones breaking away from the cartilage in the water, or those long beautiful tail feathers plucked and falling into a pile on the kitchen floor. That afternoon, when Kitako emerged from the kitchen offering steaming bowls of the broth and soba noodles, with a bit of fresh daikon radish grated on top, Uesugi and Mamoru and Wataru, the dog boy, hovered in the doorway like starving animals and followed her to the table, sitting down and slurping the soup immediately. They made moans of pleasure. *Oishii!*—"Isn't it delicious?" Morie shook his head and refused a bowl. He demanded another glass of sake instead.

"I just couldn't eat it," he says. "I have never been able to eat anything that I've killed. It's hard to explain. I haven't given it much thought, but I don't think it's about guilt over killing. It just seems a natural reaction. But Kitako was happy to have pheasant, or anything else I brought home, and so was my family."

Whether he ate or not, he'd found it exhilarating—having hunted and returned, fed and provided—and exciting to be with Uesugi in the mountains, walking with him through the groves of ancient cedars, following his routes and learning his favorite spots, viewing the dam and the Hanayama wilderness through the *matagi*'s eyes. As the years passed and Morie became a frequent companion of the professional hunter, and an informal apprentice of sorts, he was honored every time Uesugi invited him out. The *matagi* taught him how to camp in the snow, build a fire in a heavy wind, how to make his own bullets with molten lead. Morie tried not to make a fool of himself, or show any arrogance. He stayed quiet and paid close attention. Everything about Uesugi intrigued and impressed him: the way he walked in the snow with just his socks inside a pair of snowshoes, the way he never seemed to get lost, even without a map or compass. He didn't travel on cleared paths—he made his own, sometimes swinging from trees or pole-vaulting over rivers and swamps with long branches stuck into the muddy banks.

Depending on the conditions of the snow—wet or dry or icy or crusty, slick or watery, thin or deep—Uesugi had a different pair of snowshoes, each made out of bent wood that was tied with vines, looking something like a wicker basket. There were special shoes for hiking in the mountains, and another pair for the woods. "For hunting, the right snowshoe is as important as the bullet," he liked to say. He showed Morie how to cut the wood, steam and soften it—shaping it exactly for his height and weight. If the snowshoe wasn't right, you could wind up in trouble.

Uesugi had all kinds of rules and theories, and collected wisdom about the mountains that Morie found invaluable. But more than anything, Morie found it liberating to be in the company of a person who lived so differently from everybody else, so outside the norm—particularly in Japan, where a reverence for uniformity prevailed, where the beauty and elegance of sameness and predictability was honored. Homogeneity was an essential quality of being Japanese, almost an accomplishment, a virtue of the highest standard. As schoolchildren everyone was taught "the stake that sticks up gets hammered down." Morie's memories of childhood were mostly of being in a cluster of siblings who were obeying or giving implicit signals and commands to fit in. The team was important, not you. It worked so well for most people. It seemed to work for Kitako, who made many sacrifices for the children and the family, and who wanted the things her sisters had, things that city people all wanted, and it would probably work as well for Morie's children, who had been raised by the society around them, by a force so strong and solid and harmonious that they seemed, almost overnight, to have grown up into trees in a forest of identical trees.

The children seemed embarrassed by their father. They winced at his loud voice, and the heavy Akita accent, and probably at his collection of hats and berets, too. Like Kitako, the children wished that he was like the other Mitsubishi dads, the corporate executives who played golf and relaxed on the weekend, counting the days before they could retire to a warmer climate.

Uesugi never talked about his own childhood, or parents, or siblings, or anything he'd experienced prior to retreating into the deep woods and becoming a *matagi* apprentice at twenty-two. His life began then, swept clean. He'd joined a tribe of hunters and started himself over again—or discovered what he was really meant to be. He was raw, unspoiled, and stronger than all the pressures to conform. As soon as he could, he had even left the society of other *matagi*. "I have to live on my own," he had told Morie. He had never owned a car or television, never made plans more than a day ahead or bothered to save money. If you were sick, he'd give you all his wild ginseng, or whatever *kumanoi* he had left, and as soon as he killed a bear, he sold it and spent the money that night—drinking and gambling—which made him very popular with local people everywhere. As kind and generous as he was with people in town, or Kitako, and the children as they grew up, Uesugi cared only about today, not tomorrow—and lived in the moment more than anybody Morie had ever met.

Sometimes Morie dreamt of such a life—of being alone, living with the animals, knowing all the secrets of the mountains. He wanted to be able to survive in the wild by skill and intelligence and awareness and *kishō*. Maybe all the things that he looked for in his dogs were things that he wanted in himself, or wanted to encourage, and keep alive in the face of the changing requirements of modern life.

"Uesugi-san was unique: the most fascinating person I've ever known," Morie says. "He was leading a life that would have been anybody's dream. Total freedom. And when I was with him, I became aware of how much I wasn't like other people—that I wasn't normal either. And I knew I didn't want to become soft and spoiled by modern convenience."

When Dr. Sato came to the village of Masaka to build a three-story private hospital, Morie was very pleased. A new hospital was a sign of success and progress, and reflected well upon everyone in the region. In addition, Dr. Sato was a serious and sober fellow, the patriarch of a small but accomplished family. His wife was a sophisticated woman who'd been raised in Tokyo—and Kitako quickly made friends with her. Dr. Sato's only child, Yumi, was demure and intelligent and pretty, and Mamoru, then fifteen, became her friend. For his part, Morie admired Dr. Sato, but the two men were never close. Sato was stocky and athletic, a former kendo master with shiny dark hair, thick eyebrows, white skin, and a terrible allergy to alcohol. He didn't drink anything but green tea. That was the basic problem. "If you can't drink with somebody," Morie likes to say, "it's hard to know them well." Also, as much as Sato liked dogs and kept them, the hospital was his great passion—not Akitas. It was this, along with his teetotaling, that made him dull company for Morie. But Sato's X-ray technician, Wataru Ito, was an entirely different story.

Wataru lived at the hospital and worked for Dr. Sato until early afternoon, when his real life began: being with Morie's dogs. Wataru was crazy for dogs, perhaps the most dog-centric person Morie had ever met. He was just a young kid really—only seventeen or eighteen—when he'd turned up at Morie's kennel the first time.

Like Victory Princess, he was a stray with a problem. He was a handsome kid, strong and hearty, but he had a chronic stutter.

His father was Masutaro Ito, the mayor of the Akita village of Shimizu and Morie's dignified old dog friend from way back. When it became obvious Wataru was something of a misfit, and not college material, Masutaro had called Morie asking for his help. The idea was that Wataru could be trained as an apprentice X-ray technician at Dr. Sato's hospital and acquire an expertise that would be useful, and profitable, for the rest of his life.

The problem was, Wataru wasn't much interested in X-raying sick patients. He only cared about dogs. He'd been showing his father's Akitas in the dog ring and advising the farmers of Shimizu since he was a schoolboy. Even on days when he was supposed to be working at the hospital, he'd wind up driving over in Dr. Sato's hospital car to see Morie, to have a cup of sake and play with Victory and her puppies. Wataru was very *tanuki*, or raccoon-like, as they say in Japan—cute, fun, noisy, mischievous, but not too smart. Everybody liked having him around, and before long, it was a rare night when Wataru wasn't sitting at the dinner table with Mamoru, like a third brother. And after dinner, he would linger until Morie's other buddies showed up to drink and talk dogs.

Wataru loved dog talk—a mixture of debate, analysis, handicapping, and prognostication. But when he grew tense or excited, his stutter worsened and, combined with his Akita accent, there were times when he was simply impossible to comprehend. Kitako would calm him. "Slow down, relax, *take your time*," she'd say. Morie had his own methods of dealing with Wataru's affliction. When his stutter became painful to hear, Morie just poured him another drink. Wataru loved sake. It soothed him, and allowed him to express himself.

He wasn't the average dog boy, in any case—no lackey or yes-man

Wataru in the ring, still in his school uniform

to Morie. On afternoons and weekends, he moved into the house and took over the dog operation. Wataru was a handler, trainer, and breeder. He had his own opinions and plans, his own deals and schemes. He was an all-around fixer who made arrangements for stud services and show-ring fees. And when he wasn't busy selling puppies for the farmers in Shimizu—where Hoko was still fathering prize-winning dogs—Wataru was wrangling and wheedling and making side deals to ensure that his favorite customers and friends got all the best puppies from Morie's litters.

Victory Princess was the reigning bitch of that era—fertile and always pregnant or nursing or recovering from both. Her puppies were wonderful, one batch after another, almost like magic. Their coats were thick, their ears were always perfect—nobody had seen such gorgeously erect ears—and their *kishō* was magnificent too. Quite a few of them had already done brilliantly in the show ring, so when Victory had another litter coming, Wataru kept the dog-vine on edge with dispatches.

Wataru and Morie spent a great deal of time talking about Victory in those days, and imagining which stud dog would give her the finest puppies. Each winter, after many bottles of sake, and many long nights of conversation, they would choose a new mate for her. And every winter they'd choose a different male dog. All the litters had turned out well. But when Victory was about seven years old, something extraordinary occurred. Wataru and Morie seemed to stumble upon the perfect stud for her: Leather Water, a fine black-and-white male who was a few years younger.

Victory was always a little weird about her puppies—and fiercely protective. The family made jokes about the way she guarded her little ones, nursing them obsessively, and snapping or growling if anybody got within a few feet of them. When she gave birth, like

Ryoko and Happiness

other Akitas, she'd dig a hole in the ground just big enough for her body. She made a lot of noise when she delivered—howled for hours—and cut the umbilical cords by biting them with her teeth. Other bitches allowed Morie to cut the cords and touch their puppies as soon as they were born. But Victory made it difficult to examine the litters until the pups were older, and ready to be weaned, at which time Morie removed them very carefully from her clutches and took them to his special puppy coop. Handling Victory's puppies was always a little dangerous, and the family joked about it, but Morie didn't think Victory deserved the derision. "Don't make fun of her," he said. "She knows what she's doing. Just leave her alone!"

With this sixth litter of puppies bred with Leather Water, Morie could see that they were all spectacular, but right away, one of the little bitches stood out immediately. She was black and white, like her father, and her eyes were sweet. She was also confident, energetic, and seemed to hold herself differently from the others, as if she knew she was special. Even when she was just six or eight weeks old, she seemed unusually brave and, at the same time, gentle and loving. Kitako kept eyeing the puppy too. "She had a spark and balance, and a feeling of immense calm." Kitako asked to name her Happiness.

As time passed, and the other pups in the litter were given away— or traded for next year's stud fee—Happiness became only lovelier and more secure, as if growing into her name. And from the moment she entered the dog ring as a six-month-old puppy, she never did anything but win and win again. At the smaller regional shows in Miyagi prefecture, where there still weren't too many Akitas, taking first prize wasn't so difficult. But when Morie took Happiness to the national competitions in Odate, she won there too. She was strong and solid, but sweet and biddable. And in a time of great excitement about Akitas—when the prices for them had inflated almost as

Mamoru walking
Victory and Happiness

much as Tokyo real estate—Happiness became a champion in Odate so many times that several judges told Morie that the dog was very close to entering the Akita Preservation Society's Hall of Fame, a lifetime achievement that would remove her from further competition.

On the date of the next big spring show, May 3, Morie had an important meeting at the power plant and couldn't go. Hating to miss an opportunity to take Happiness to Odate, where she might be awarded a Hall of Fame award and where dog people from all over Japan would see her, Morie asked Gisuke Yamamoto, a longtime dog buddy from Hachimantai, to show the dog in his place. Just walk her out into the ring and she will win, Morie told Yamamoto. The dog was looking better than ever. Happiness had been outside hunting and exercising all winter and her fur was spectacularly thick and full. Also, she was robust and ready to be bred. That was Morie's other wish: At the big show, a suitable stud might appear.

Dog news could travel fast, but in those days, not as fast as one might think. A day after the big show, Morie started to wonder how things had gone and waited for Yamamoto to appear and give him a report. Yamamoto was a nice enough guy, but vain and a little flaky, maybe a little damaged. He'd spent years in a prisoner-of-war camp in Siberia—Morie had helped him find work when he'd been released. As the days passed, and various dog buddies began to report on which dogs had won at the big show, and which dogs had lost, Morie still heard no word from Yamamoto. He assumed that he'd taken Happiness back to Hachimantai and had been delayed—possibly by illness or accident—but since Yamamoto had no telephone, it wasn't so unusual not to have heard from him. After a week, though, Morie asked Kitako to make some phone calls and see what she could find out. She heard various accounts, each more upsetting than the last.

Apparently Yamamoto had been overwhelmed by the attention that Happiness had gotten in Odate, even before the show began. The weather had been incredible, warm and clear, and the cherry blossoms were out. Like everybody else during cherry blossom time, Yamamoto had been drinking a good deal, and appreciating life and the good weather. The circumference of the park where the show ring was set up was full of vendors selling food and sake. Everywhere Yamamoto walked with Happiness, he was complimented on her. Nobody had ever seen such a beautiful dog! And under the blue skies and white puffy clouds, and by the boughs of blossoming cherry trees, Yamamoto was approached by a very dignified man from the south. He wanted to know if Happiness was for sale. The man said he was willing to pay ten million yen for such a magnificent dog. It was enough money to buy a pretty nice house.

Yamamoto went to the Akita Preservation Society office, across from the park, forged the registry documents, and sold Happiness to the man. On the documents, the buyer's name was Ota, a shipbuilder in Osaka.

Before long, Kitako and Morie's phone was ringing. Was it true? Had Yamamoto really sold Happiness? The next morning, a call came from Osaka. The shipbuilder, Ota, had been informed by a fellow Akita breeder that the dog he'd purchased had been stolen. "I am so sorry, so terribly sorry," Ota told Kitako on the phone. "I am mortified. Please allow me to return the dog to you."

"But you have paid good money for her," Kitako said.

"But she is your dog," Ota said.

The next day, Ota and his wife flew into Sendai and arrived at

Gisuke Yamamoto with
Hoko in 1960

Morie and Kitako's house to apologize in person. He was an older man, elegantly dressed, and his manners were so exquisite, it was almost painful. "I feel so ashamed," he said, "and don't want to become party to a crime."

"I was so moved by his apologies," Morie says, "I told him to please keep Happiness. He wasn't to blame. He had done nothing wrong. And I knew that now, after all this, he would appreciate the dog even more. What a fine man Ota-san was—I could see that. And I realized how much I wanted to make friends with a man as fine as he was."

They struck an agreement quickly: Happiness would return to Morie the following year and have a litter of puppies at his house, under his expert supervision. Morie would keep one of the puppies and afterward, Happiness would be returned to Osaka. At that time, Mr. Ota promised to show Morie and Kitako around Kyoto.

Kitako was particularly excited by this last offer. It had been one of her lifelong dreams to see the old imperial city. And the following year, when it came time to return Happiness and visit the Ota family, Kitako went by herself. She still talks about the wonderful trip to Kyoto—and how Morie stayed home with the dogs. While sightseeing around the beautiful city of Kyoto, she also had a very pleasant visit with Mrs. Ota, who made many inquiries about Kitako's children and where they were going to school. Kitako was very proud, in particular, of her very talented daughter Ryoko, who was the only woman in her class at veterinary school. It hadn't been easy for her to be accepted at that school. Mitsubishi paid for part of her tuition, but the cost was still very steep and the family had made sacrifices.

Kitako downplayed the difficulties. The truth was, she owed money at nearly all the shops in town and had pressured Morie to borrow heavily against his retirement in order to pay bills and tuition. She didn't feel Mrs. Ota needed to know all the details, but whatever she said, Mrs. Ota understood—and action was taken. "My mother never told me the story directly," Ryoko says. "All I knew was that somehow a very rich man had helped with my school tuition and that my mother had gone to him many times and asked to borrow money. But he wouldn't hear of a loan. He only wanted to give it. And that's how I got through school."

As for Morie, he never knew what had transpired between Kitako and the Ota family, or much of anything, except that Ota-san was his friend for life, and a marvelous man who appreciated dogs, and who had known Morie's generosity. To him, this exchange was more than fair.

As for Yamamoto? Morie refused to notify the police. "Thieves and liars suffer their own punishments in life," he says. "I did the right thing." And forty-five years later, when Morie heard that Yamamoto experienced a terribly painful death, he wasn't surprised. It was a "cheater's death," Morie says. "That's what he deserves for stealing Happiness."

Seven

Samurai Tiger

In old Japan, there was a type of warrior who trained with mountain dogs. They lived with dogs to study their boldness and spirit—how these led them into confrontations that seemed impossible to win, but then how their cunning instincts enabled them to dominate beasts much larger and stronger: they cornered bears and harried them with nonstop barking until the bears would lose their heads and do stupid things, or things that evened the odds. The samurai believed the snow country dogs possessed a special instinct for martial arts, as well as a unique temperament that could be emulated. It wasn't raw aggression that kept them alive in the heat of battle. The dogs had a kind of absolute devotion, a selflessness, which gave them power and miraculous endurance. They fought with gaping wounds and broken limbs and shreds of fur hanging from their bodies. They fought, and kept fighting, with a spirit that seemed more than anything their bodies could contain, and often without a whimper.

To Morie, those old legends sometimes seemed distorted or exaggerated. By 1970, he had raised enough dogs to believe that he knew the range of their abilities, and the limits. But then Samurai Tiger raised the bar.

IT HAD BEEN YEARS since Morie had judged for the Akita Preservation Society or sat on the board. He'd given up his position due to lack of time, and the fact that, increasingly, he felt out of sync with the goals of the group. Their aspirations, he felt, were largely about winning prizes and making money. Morie loved winning prizes—no denying that—but as he spent more time in the mountains, hunting with Uesugi every spring and fall, he suspected there was a divide between the beautiful dogs that won in the ring and those with any canine spirit to speak of.

How it had happened was understandable. When the exhibitions started again in 1946, the few Akita dogs who had survived World War II were so uneven physically that the emphasis of the preservation society, as well as the other Akita clubs that sprang up, had been to breed dogs for a specific appearance—upright ears, a tightly curled tail, a wider face, a shorter snout. Morie didn't disagree with the effort to return the Akita to a more authentic look and to eliminate the effects of crossbreeding. But in the rush toward conformity—and the effort to produce an Akita that looked like a traditional Akita and not a German shepherd—the interior qualities of the classic snow country dog had gone missing.

As far as Morie could tell, the instincts of each generation of dogs was weaker than the last. Other breeders didn't seem much concerned. When Happiness had her puppies, the Ota family was enormously pleased with them, and many of the dogs went on to win prizes, but no samurai would have wanted to train with those lovely creatures. They had nice shapes and good color, but they were languid beauties with low energy. They were as passive as Morie's laid-back champion Shinonome. It bothered Morie that this sort of dog could dominate in the show ring but wasn't good for much else.

What Morie wanted in a dog was a "strong sense of the core traits—an instinct that helps him find the weakness in his enemy. So if you face a bear in the mountains, the dog knows automatically without being taught to go behind the bear. It's that kind of survival instinct that kept the Akita alive for centuries—an unconscious intelligence, even brilliance," Morie says. "It took ten years of waiting for Happiness to come and what a fine dog she was. But her puppies bothered me a little. There were problems with their ears too. Genetics is complicated—and looking back, I have been more often frustrated than rewarded."

He needed a hunting dog. That was the main thing. Victory Princess was getting old and it seemed wrong to ask her to hunt in stressful conditions. "She loved the mountains, and always wanted to come out with me," Morie says, "but I started to worry it wasn't safe for her."

In the fall of 1967, he heard good things about a litter of puppies on a farm outside of Odate. Morie went to see them and invited Uesugi along. The *matagi* claimed to know a reliable method for selecting a good hunting dog and Morie was curious. Unlike his other friends, Uesugi wasn't a dog nut. He didn't care about Akitas or any other specific "breed." Sometimes Uesugi gave Morie a hard time about his fixation with what seemed an arbitrary standard, the sixty-seven qualities and traits that were supposed to come together in one dog in order to deem it acceptable. "Uesugi just wanted a good hunting dog," Morie says, "and never cared what it looked like."

Morie had favorite techniques for testing the temperament of a

Mr. and Mrs. Ota were thrilled with
Happiness's puppies, but Morie wasn't

puppy that came from another kennel—things he'd used in the past. He never picked a puppy that cried or whined or seemed nervous. Sometimes he was interested in whether a puppy bullied his littermates—a sign of boldness and dominance—but there wasn't a test for strength and courage, or hunting instincts, as far as he knew. "Some people just want a beautiful Akita and don't care if it knows anything, or if it's strong and fearless," Morie says. "They want the dog just to admire and appreciate for its looks, a dog that's simply a recipient of their affection. For them, picking a puppy is a little easier. They could just pat a pretty puppy and see if its tail wagged. That's a sign of agreeability, of wanting to please, and a very telling response."

Looking over the puppies at the farm, Morie liked their color—they had thick black and white coats—but otherwise he felt the dogs weren't impressive. "They seemed like weaklings actually," he says. "Their faces were much too sweet." Uesugi had a different approach. "He grabbed one of the puppies very quickly by its tail and started to lift it off the ground." Morie was shocked.

"It seemed cruel," he says, "and maybe it is a little bit cruel—but he picked up the puppy very quickly and the dog arched its back and put out its paws. Uesugi said if a puppy did that, it was strong. But if the puppy squirms or cries, or whimpers or barks, then it wasn't. It's not really as cruel as it sounds, because it happens in an instant. A strong dog will remain firm. You can even hold a strong dog by its tail—lift it off the ground—and it won't complain. It will just stretch its legs out, push forward at you, and not retreat. A puppy will respond instantly and give you the information you need. It may be as simple as pain threshold. You don't want a dog with a low pain threshold. A dog that's overly sensitive will always be complaining.

"What surprised me," Morie says, "is that this fragile weakling, this sweet-faced puppy, didn't cry or whine. I was kind of astonished so I grabbed the same puppy—I couldn't resist—and when I lifted it by the tail, he did the same thing for me too. But when the owner saw me touching his dog this way, he wasn't happy. You can't really blame him. I offered to buy a puppy right there. He agreed, but only if I took two puppies. So I did. A male and a female. We called them Samurai Tiger and Shogun Princess. And as soon as I got home, I tried to decide whether to train them for hunting or the show ring. It was impossible to do both at the same time. Uesugi had made me think they were going to be good hunters, but I thought they might succeed in the ring too."

Morie deliberated over the fall, spending many nights in heated discussions with Wataru, his opinionated dog boy. They sat around the table after dinner, pouring each other beer and sake, deciding the fate of the puppies. The male was a slightly more promising dog, and clearly dominant. But was he going to the ring or hunting?

As an experiment, Morie decided to go duck hunting with Samurai Tiger, about seven months old at the time, and see how he did.

"We walked up to a pond where several ducks were swimming," Morie says. "I like to get a dog used to water early, since Akitas aren't known to be great water dogs—many of them don't like the water at all. Sometimes it takes me quite a while to get a young dog to cross a stream or river, but once I train them to do it, they'll cross all right, but won't go freely into the water on their own, without urging, until they are two or three years old.

"Also, with a young dog, you have to get them accustomed to the sound of the gun. That first day of hunting with Samurai Tiger, every time I shot at a duck, he retreated. I tried to encourage him to go in for the ducks that I'd shot, who were still struggling in the water, but he was too scared. Finally I took my shirt off and went into the water myself. And pretty soon, Tiger followed me in."

Morie praised the dog as much as he could, and then waited for Samurai Tiger to take a duck in his mouth. "An Akita doesn't like the smell of duck naturally—duck really stinks to them. Maybe all dogs hate the smell of duck, I don't know. But if you want to duck hunt with an Akita, you have to do a little extra work to get around their natural aversion to the smell. When Tiger followed me into the water, he grabbed one of the ducks in his mouth, but I think the stink was too awful and he started to drop it immediately. I praised him up and down, as much appreciation as I could possibly give him, just for picking up the duck and for coming in the water out of loyalty for me. Then I sliced open the duck, and gave him some of the liver to taste. Well, he loved it. So I gave him more. He was a terrific hunting companion after that, and never hesitated again. When I was hunting, he always wanted to help out."

Still, it nagged at Morie that he might own a champion Akita that had never seen the ring. Samurai Tiger was a promising hunter, but it was hard to see an opportunity pass. Morie felt torn himself. Was he more interested in showing dogs or hunting with them? In the old days of the snow country, these activities weren't at odds. But now they were—or so it seemed. Mostly out of curiosity, Morie decided to take Tiger to a regional show in Sendai to give him a taste of the ring and see how he fared. Hunting required a complex set of traits and instincts, but victories in the ring could be elusive and demanded their own blend of qualities too. Sometimes an otherwise confident dog hated the ring, and got spooked. Other dogs might suddenly appear diminished, and less interesting. But show prizes weren't solely a matter of appearance. A certain attitude was important—and the projection of strength. It was theater and the dog had to play along. "The dog's whole body has to look strong and firm, particularly the abdomen," Morie says. "The face is important too, without a doubt, and has to reflect personality."

Samurai Tiger won the regional puppy competition in Sendai and Morie was encouraged, but it was just a small show and didn't count much. What counted was the big show in Odate. It drew the top Akita breeders from all over Japan, and the top dogs. Happiness had taken first prize in Odate, as had Shinonome, and even Hoko. But Morie couldn't predict what the judges were looking for anymore. Talking about this one night, he and Wataru hatched a plan.

To help Samurai Tiger's chances as much as he could, Morie decided that he wouldn't make an appearance in Odate. Instead, he'd send his son Mamoru in his place. When Mamoru heard the news, he complained. What? *Why me?* He was seventeen and more interested in spending a day with Dr. Sato's daughter, Yumi, than in showing his father's dogs. Why couldn't Wataru go?

Morie explained the reasoning: If Mamoru walked the dogs around the park in Odate before the show, he would get an honest reaction from the dog crowd—people would feel comfortable approaching the young man and expressing their opinions about Samurai Tiger. If Wataru or Morie went, people would be much more threatened, and therefore hesitant. But even more important, "my dad said if he sent me, and didn't come himself," Mamoru says, "it was a way to send a signal that Samurai Tiger was such a spectacular puppy that even his teenage son couldn't ruin the dog's chances with inexperienced handling."

By 1968, Morie knew the dog crowd as well as he knew dogs. In Odate, Mamoru was besieged by breeders and handlers, dog nuts and dog wannabes, all wanting to know the details about his father's new eight-month-old puppy. Nobody had seen such a handsome, strong dog. You could see its muscles under its tight coat, and when the dog stood in the ring, his barrel chest stuck out. Had Morie taught the dog to stand that way? As soon as he got into the ring, the dog urinated on the ground to mark territory, and when he was walked within five yards of another Akita, he growled with such intensity, the dog boys backed off.

Samurai Tiger didn't love the ring the way some dogs do. Even better, he seemed completely above it. He won the highest prize in the puppy class that year in Odate, and in the fall, he won the young dog class too. He was the rare dog who could both show and hunt. He'd cornered two bears on the mountain by the time he was awarded the title "Best in Japan," when he was two years old. In 1970, he entered the Hall of Fame. The prizes were rewarding to Morie— perhaps the things he cared about in his dogs mattered to the rest of the Akita crowd too—but even more, he was just happy for Samurai Tiger. The dog had a spirit and eagerness, and strength and boundless affection, that moved Morie. He felt honored to even possess such an incredible animal, much less be loved by him.

"They say you only get one dog in your lifetime like Samurai Tiger. He inspired me, and rewarded all my efforts over the years. He was so natural, and raw, and unspoiled. For me, he was everything I could ask for in a dog. And he had all the traits I hoped to someday see in myself too."

MORIE AND KITAKO had moved to Kurikoma by then—not an unwelcome change but an abrupt one. Mitsubishi had built a dam in the wilderness at the foot of Mount Kurikoma, deeper into Miyagi prefecture, and a hydroelectric plant was being built. Since Morie was planning to retire in the next few years the company had hired a younger man to oversee the project. He seemed like a hard worker and a sensible guy, but after a late-night scandal—a drunk driving accident involving a geisha—Mitsubishi, hoping to avoid any bad publicity, quietly discharged the man from his plant duties and Morie was asked to step in. In some ways it was a retiring man's fantasy, getting to step in to save the day. Morie liked that.

And besides, Kurikoma was a wild and beautiful spot where he and Uesugi had gone hunting quite often. Uesugi roamed the Kurikoma mountains and woods as a forest inspector, and often claimed it was one of the nicest regions in all Japan. He'd even led an expedition to the top of Mount Kurikoma where he'd planted a marker. He'd made the difficult day-long hike with two cows to haul the heavy post, two men to oversee the cows, four men to dig the hole, and two forest "officials" to stand around and watch. "I would have preferred to go alone," Uesugi explained to Morie, but "digging and carrying are not my jobs."

On short notice, the only company house available for Morie and Kitako in Kurikoma was small—just two bedrooms—but once they'd moved in, Kitako grew to like it. The house was well designed, new, and about twenty minutes from town, where there was a fish market, shops, and things to do. "Life was a little better in Kurikoma," Kitako says. "There was a road near our house, and a city not too far away. There was a bus, a hospital, and less snow. Akita is so deep into the mountains—and twenty-two hours by train to Tokyo. In Kurikoma, we were now only ten hours away. And it might as well have been ten years ahead of Akita, in terms of civilization and technical progress."

The farther away she got from Akita, the better. When Kitako thought about her early married life, so difficult, and her move to the

Uesugi is wearing the white hat

snow country, such a shock, it seemed like one long blur of difficulties and sorrows. Looking back, it was always winter, always dark, and she was always trying to keep the house warm and the children fed. She and Morie never talked about Manchuria—ever—or the last days of the war, or the babies they'd lost, or even Three Good Lucks. When Kitako gathered with her sisters and their families, they never spoke of the war either. They talked about how sweet the persimmon tasted this year, or how full the blossoms were in spring, or how much better the future was looking. As for Kitako, along with the deprivations of the past, she preferred to forget Akita prefecture too. "You read about northern Japan and the harsh life there," she says, "but if you live there, you know it's even more difficult, and reflected in the attitude of its people. It's a solemn place."

Once again Kitako had found herself in a new house, a new village, but this time, the kids were no longer around. Atsuko had married Noritsugu Fukushima and was working as a schoolteacher just south of Tokyo. Ryoko was finishing veterinary school. Moritake had gone to China to work as an apprentice chef. Young Mamoru—a bit of a troublemaker—had been sent to a private boarding school nearby and only came home on weekends. "Those first years in Kurikoma," Kitako says, "Morie and I were really all alone. It was the first time since we'd been married." Kitako did feel lonely, but something else too—a wistful feeling, almost beautiful, as though a part of her was waking up. She had begun to appreciate things she'd not noticed before, mountain things, the way the morning air smelled when the warm sunlight hit the earth, the way the shadows of the treetops danced on a windy afternoon. She loved the trickle of the creek behind their small house, and how the water bounced on its rocky bed. There was a solemn austerity to life in the mountains, and yet . . . a fullness of spirit.

In the morning when the dogs bolted from their kennels and followed Morie into the woods, it seemed as though they were disappearing to a magical land, to another time. Their territory seemed boundless, miles and miles of green meadows, forests of towering cedars, and mountain peaks with sheer cliffs. The dogs craved the wild, Morie always said. It kept their instincts sharp, their spirits strong. It kept them from complacency and spiritual decline. Being in the wild reminded them who they really were—and the amazing deeds they were meant for. It was an antidote to the convenience and comfort of modern life. Kitako wondered if people didn't need the wild too.

She wasn't completely alone with Morie, though. Wataru Ito continued to live and work at Dr. Sato's clinic during the week but saved his free time and almost all of his energy for Morie and the dogs. The better Morie's dogs did in the ring, the more fanatical Wataru became. Morie let him manage the kennel and breeding operations, as well as handle the dogs at the smaller shows, and compensated Wataru with meals and sake, a place to sleep whenever needed, and lots and lots of puppies—often from Victory or Happiness, who kept returning to Morie's to have more litters. As a result, Wataru's wheeling and dealing grew more intense and mysterious, and his self-importance escalated. Before long he had a very active side business going—raising his puppies at Dr. Sato's, winning prizes with them, and then selling them off for impossibly high prices. Wataru tended to like pretty Akitas with long skinny legs, foxlike heads, and slanted eyes. And while these dogs didn't appeal to Morie, it was amazing how successful Wataru was at selling them, as well as Samurai Tiger's offspring. He walked around with more cash on hand than Morie. The family joked that the show ring success of Samurai Tiger had gone to Wataru's head because sometimes he wasn't quite so charming and *tanuki* anymore. He acted more like the King of the Dog Boys, and maybe he was.

As for Samurai Tiger, the dog was so glorious and strong, there seemed to be a field of sensuous energy around him. After so many years, and so many dogs, Kitako marveled how one of them could stand out so much—and change their lives. People came from all over the north to see him, or ask for his puppies. People appeared on bikes, driving motorcycles, they came in trucks and vans. They pulled up the driveway and stood at the front door. Have any puppies? And inside the house, the conversation over dinner, or afterward, often gravitated to Tiger stories, Tiger jokes, Tiger observations. Even Uesugi treated the dog like a celebrity. Once, when Samurai Tiger was tired after two days of hunting, and had an important exhibition to attend, Uesugi gave him wild ginseng to boost his energy. It worked so well, the dog shook with excitement on the morning of the show—but by the time he was meant to enter the ring, he was sound asleep.

Tiger was strong but soft, and always eager to please Morie. Kitako found it amusing how the dog always gravitated to her husband. But when she thought about it, Samurai Tiger and the rest of the dogs were just one circle of life around Morie. There was so much circling around him—hunters, mountain types, lovers of dogs, lovers of the wild. They were a passionate bunch and their tales over dinner and sake were full of adventure and mystery. By comparison Kitako felt like a hen cooped up on a nest.

"I'd like to start hunting," she said to Morie one night. "I want you to teach me how to shoot a gun."

Morie stared at her.

"I'm tired," she said, "of you having all the fun."

She passed the test to obtain a gun permit and a gun, answering questions about types of bullets and safety rules. The desk officer at the police department said she was the only woman who had ever taken the test, as far as he knew. When she came home with the permit, and a brand-new shotgun from a shop in Sendai, Morie got a large sheet of white canvas, ten feet square, and painted a series of concentric circles on it in black paint, with a dot in the middle. He wasn't going into the mountains with Kitako until she'd had a lot of target practice.

He found her a pair of hiking boots, and a waterproof hunting jacket. She came up with the rest of her mountain outfit, which included a wide-brimmed hat. "I tried to look feminine," she says. Morie seemed a little rattled the first time Kitako held the gun. There was a moment when he showed her how to reload it, and beads of sweat broke out on his face.

Their first morning out together, they walked into the woods and Morie began to teach her things he'd learned from Uesugi or the other hunters. Kitako seemed adept, almost immediately, at rabbit hunting. And this unnerved Morie a bit. He lectured her on the hazards of rabbit hunting, namely how you shouldn't chase a rabbit unless you were willing to get very lost. The secret about mountain rabbits is that they always hop and feed in a circle, he said, and eventually return to the same spot. So if you lose sight of one, just stand still for twenty minutes and the rabbit will be back.

She loved hunting pheasants and smaller mountain birds in the autumn and rabbits in the snow—when only the tips of their ears are visible—and often did better than Morie. Uesugi asked her along with him quite often. Other times, she joined a group of Kurikoma hunters that Morie had met. She liked hunting in a group. In front of other people, Morie wasn't so critical of her. "I think we were very competitive, that's all," says Kitako. "If just the two of us went bird hunting or rabbit hunting, he'd say: 'Stand there!' And then he'd put himself in a much better place, moving himself into the ideal position. And if I shot a rabbit first, he'd say, 'That was a lucky shot.' His forestry buddies and hunting buddies asked me to hunt with them and were much nicer."

"Actually, I didn't like her coming with me," Morie says. "She walks slower than I do and it exhausted me. But I don't want to get into a fight right here, talking about it."

No matter: Kitako loved the feeling of stepping into a wild place, being surrounded by green in the summer, gold and orange and red in the autumn, and white in winter. She loved the morning sunlight and fresh air, learning to shoot, and bringing home something to skin and cook. She felt proud to be able to keep up with Morie, and ford creeks or swing over rushing streams by hanging on a vine like Tarzan. She liked being in the mountains with Uesugi, too, and relished being able to join in the hunting talk with the men. "There was no point in thinking about Tokyo after I started going into the mountains," she says. "It was soothing to be surrounded by nature, by snow in the winter, the soba flowers flickering, and to have experiences to recount later."

Besides, her mountain life soon would be coming to an end. Salarymen in Japan were retiring in their fifties now to make room for the next generation of salarymen. In 1969, Morie turned fifty-three. Mitsubishi had asked him to stay on as long as he could to see the Kurikoma project completed—at least another four or five years. But after that, Kitako imagined she'd be saying good-bye to the mountains. Maybe learning to hunt was her way of doing that.

"I still wanted a more civilized life, a city life," she says, "but I remember wondering if we had enough money to live in Tokyo again. And I wondered where we'd walk the dogs."

. . .

SAMURAI TIGER was two years old when he first went bear hunting. Uesugi appeared unexpectedly one night and said he'd found a bear cave on the mountain above Morie's house. "Let's go hunting in the morning," he said to Morie. The spring thaw was the traditional time for bear hunting—when the bears came out of hibernation, grumpy and hungry—but this was the middle of December.

Excited and nervous, Morie spent the rest of the evening packing for the hunting trip. He told Kitako that they'd be gone two or three days and would need only dried herring and *onigiri* or rice balls to eat. Over the years, Uesugi had talked a lot about bear hunting, told the stories of his apprenticeship with his *matagi* master, and always pointed out bear dung and prints when he saw them in the woods. Bears were his livelihood and his passion, really, but until Morie came along, Uesugi always hunted them alone. He carried a *Murata-ju,* a long single-barreled shotgun designed for military use at the turn of the century. He didn't believe in using double-barreled rifles or automatic weapons of any kind. One shot was all he ever allowed himself. "It makes the fight fair," he liked to say. Usually, after cornering and killing a bear in the mountains, he cut out the gallbladder for himself and left the rest of the fallen animal in the forest. He'd head down the mountain to one of several larger villages and sell the body of the bear sight unseen. The meat, bones, claws, organs, and pelt— every part of the bear could be resold and used. Uesugi drew strange pictographs and maps of the mountain with various markers showing where to find the bear's body. It was one of the things you'd hear about Uesugi in the village, how miraculously detailed his maps of the mountain were, and how precise and easy the directions were to follow.

On the morning of Morie's first bear hunt, he and Uesugi rose before dawn and walked in the snow to the other side of the Tamagawa Hot Springs on the way to Lake Tazawa in the snow, about eight or nine miles away. They brought Samurai Tiger along, but since he had never hunted a bear before—or smelled one—he wouldn't be able to help them track. That was left to Uesugi. "Samurai Tiger and I had never hunted bear before, or even tried," Morie says. "Uesugi always said that when you stood face-to-face with a bear, it brought out the true nature of a dog and the true nature of a man."

Even though some of the old legends about Akitas describe them hunting in pairs, Morie never hunted with more than one dog. He found that his dogs tended to compete for game and fights started. There were other displays of dominance, too, which were distracting and simply a waste of time. Uesugi and Morie held the same view on this: one good dog was more than enough. An Akita with good hunting instincts would stalk large game like bear by slinking low to the ground, almost catlike, and creeping slowly toward its prey. Once it got closer, the dog circled the prey and bayed at it, detaining it until the hunter could approach. If the bear tried to escape, the dog closed off routes of escape and sometimes leapt on the bear's neck and latched on with its teeth. The dog would hang on to the bear's neck until the hunter arrived and took it down.

Beyond the hot springs, the men walked up to the foot of the mountain and climbed up a ravine to a waterfall. "Near the falls, on the wet ground, there was an old stump of an oak tree," Morie says. "The trunk had a curved area—a rotted-out hole at the bottom. It didn't look like a very big hole to me, just one foot across, but Uesugi was convinced that a bear lived inside it."

The men stood on either side of the tree stump, and Uesugi tried several ways to tempt the bear—which he was sure was there—out of the hole. He waved an oily cloth over the hole, a smell that was supposed to drive the bear out. "Then we lit the oily cloth on fire," Morie says. "It smelled like sulfur and made a lot of smoke. Uesugi-san waved it very close to the hole and then he crouched down behind the trunk with the butt of a hunting knife in his hand. I was supposed to stand there, prepared to shoot as soon as I saw the face of the bear coming out of the hole."

Morie still wasn't sure how a bear could fit in the hole, but he had learned to trust Uesugi. "He told me not to fire until two thirds of the bear had emerged. Once he'd waved the smoky cloth, and crouched down, he said the bear would be coming within ten seconds. So I held up the gun and waited."

But those ten seconds "seemed like forever," Morie says, "and my arms began to shake. I was so scared. My arms were shaking all over the place. I couldn't even keep the gun pointed. I was a hunter, but not a bear hunter! That was something else."

"Shoot in ten seconds," Uesugi whispered.

But Morie's hand wouldn't stay still and "I couldn't focus on my gun," he says. "Samurai Tiger was behind me, just watching and waiting. Then, all of a sudden, I saw a bear's tiny face. The hole was so small—it seemed way too small for anything—but in a split second, the entire bear was out of the hole. Uesugi had told me to shoot the bear's head but, to be honest, I just had to shoot whatever I could. I heard a clicking of teeth, a chattering. I didn't know if it was me or the gun.

"The bear's fur was standing on end—and that made him seem so much bigger to me," he says. "I finally pulled the trigger and I had a sense that I'd hit him, but almost instantly, he disappeared. There wasn't a bear there anymore. I thought maybe it had fallen dead, but then I realized it had just gone back in the hole. Honestly, I can't really remember exactly what happened next because it was a blur. But eventually we concluded the bear was inside the stump and probably dead. So we had to pry open the stump to get him—and that took hours."

After they'd hauled the bear out of the hole, Uesugi gave Samurai Tiger some of its blood to lap up. "That did something powerful to him," Morie says of the dog. "After that, it was as if he'd follow that scent to the ends of the earth to taste it again."

MORIE'S ATTITUDE ABOUT raising his children hadn't been much different from the way he raised his dogs, who lived outside in the winter snow in order to grow thick coats. "The more challenging the environment, the stronger the children will be," he liked to say. In many ways, he was a typical father of his era—stern, unemotional, and physically undemonstrative. Even so, Morie's four kids found it upsetting at times that he seemed to be methodically preparing them for a difficult life by giving them a difficult childhood. They struggled in their relationships with him—with varying results.

Atsuko, the oldest, had always been the most agreeable and uncomplaining. She was an elementary school teacher—responsible, organized, but also cheerful and quick to laugh. ("I used to tease her," Morie says, "that she became a schoolteacher because she knew how much I'd always hated the teachers when I was growing up.") And even though Morie had discouraged her from going to college and had wanted her to accept an arranged marriage to a professional baseball player who worked for her uncle Kinoshita, Atsuko seemed to hold no noticeable grudges. Neither did Morie. When she married her longtime boyfriend Noritsugu, the entire family was thrilled. "Nori-chan," as they affectionately called him, had a reputation for being a party boy and a bit of a goof-off. He loved his boat, playing golf, watching TV, and it had taken him longer than usual to finish college. But his own father was a strong figure, a successful businessman—the head of Mitsubishi–Reynolds Aluminum—and Noritsugu seemed to know instinctively how to get along with Morie. The Mitsubishi connection hadn't hurt either. And when the couple produced a grandchild, a gorgeous girl named Yukari, even better.

The oldest son, Moritake, looked the most like Morie and was knowledgeable about dogs, too. He did well at a private high school in Sendai for a while but appeared to buckle a bit under pressure. When he didn't pass his college boards, he left home and was out of contact with the family for four or five years until they heard he was in China learning to cook. Moritake's relationship with Ryoko had always been rocky, but it was Mamoru who seemed to irritate him the most. The two sons were five years apart and fought frequently. Morie stayed out of it, as though it were a natural thing—and almost expected—that siblings would be like two dogs vying for dominance. The truth is, Morie didn't get too involved when it came to raising the kids. He introduced them to the natural world—built tree houses and made bamboo sleds, and took them to swim in the dam. Otherwise, he had high expectations, doled out harsh criticism, but left all the nurturing to Kitako. "He was very Spartan," says Atsuko, "and not consistent in his attention."

"He never praised us much or gave us affection," remembers Mamoru, "and then we'd watch him go outside and hug the dogs."

The sons may have fought, and been neglected at times, but it was Ryoko who felt singled out for dismissal—simply for being a girl. She had a big personality, lots of energy and drive, and looked a great deal like her mother. In high school when she studied for tests

Atsuko and Noritsugu holding Yukari

over the winter, she kept her bedroom windows open and the room freezing, and wore a coat and gloves, in order to stay awake all night. She had expressed interest in becoming a medical doctor—her memory of watching two younger siblings die in the house was still vivid—but Morie refused to discuss it. ("Women shouldn't work," he'd say into the air.) When Ryoko didn't pass her tests for medical school and decided to apply to veterinary school instead, it had been Kitako who went to Nihon Veterinary University in person to make sure a woman would be permitted to attend, and then had to scrounge the money for tuition. "The dogs were as much of a priority as we were," Ryoko says. "I was jealous of the dogs. They ate rice and noodles, the same food as we did—always. And I guess that bothered me."

It seems almost impossible to be the child of a man who loves dogs as much as Morie did and not be bothered by it. "When I look back, I realize that my father made most of his friends through the dogs," Ryoko says. "They'd come to the house and drink and be together. I remember how happy my father's face was then—so happy to be with his dogs and dog buddies. That's when he was clearly happiest, much happier than when he was with the family. It was always obvious. He never tried to hide it."

As if forgetting how unsupportive he'd been to her, when Ryoko graduated from veterinary school, Morie boasted to his buddies that she'd be moving back home to become a judge for the Akita Preservation Society and he registered one of his prizewinning dogs under Ryoko's name in order to make his daughter a member. "I had a dream that she'd become the first dog show judge with a medical degree," he explains with a lingering sense of disappointment. "But she didn't want that." Ryoko went to Yokohama Medical University to work on a master's degree instead, eventually becoming a

Ryoko took things more seriously

professor there. In 1972, when she married Yasumasa Ando, the handsome captain of their college basketball team and a veterinarian himself, Morie took the ten-hour train ride down to Tokyo for the wedding and stayed long enough to see a room full of disapproving in-laws on all sides—Kitako's family didn't care much for Morie any more—and left for home an hour later. He explained that he had to get home to look after the dogs.

"My father hadn't liked my decision to stay in Yokohama and be a professor," Ryoko explains, "and he hadn't been too happy about the man I was marrying—he was a vet, also—and leaving early was his way of expressing that."

When she became pregnant the following year, though, she did come north to have the baby at Dr. Sato's hospital, and then remained in Kurikoma throughout the New Year's holiday. But from Ryoko's perspective that decision hadn't turned out well. The newborn cried at night and "all my mother did was complain about being tired," Ryoko says. "I didn't understand her, and she didn't understand me, and we didn't have much to say to each other."

Ryoko stayed at Yokohama Medical University for ten years, both teaching and running a small animal hospital. She had four children while finishing three degrees, including a Ph.D. in veterinary forensics. "By the time I graduated with my last degree, I was holding my fourth child, still a newborn, who cried throughout the whole ceremony," she says. "Everybody still makes jokes about it." She and her family moved to South Africa for a one-year research fellowship, and then to Argentina for a longer stay. It was 1985 before the family returned to Japan for good.

Mamoru has a different tale of rebellion but many of the same complaints. Fun-loving and independent-minded, often in trouble at school, Mamoru, like his father, was too stubborn to rein in easily.

Morie with Ryoko's first baby in 1973

His last semester of high school, just before taking the college boards, he was suspended for drinking and smoking. In truth, there hadn't been much discussion about college for Mamoru anyway. He was bright but restless, and never seemed to have the self-discipline that Atsuko and Ryoko had. Throughout his high school years, when he'd lived in a small dorm and commuted home on weekends, rather than studying he spent most of his free time with his first love, Yumi Sato, the daughter of Dr. Sato. It was an attraction of opposites. Yumi was sweet and introspective, a pampered only child who did well in school. She liked the Rolling Stones. Mamoru preferred the Beatles. But on weekends, they talked and shared records in Yumi's bedroom where the walls were covered with posters.

Mamoru gravitated to art and culture and dreamed of a sophisticated city life. He liked mod clothes and cool sunglasses. He loved dogs early on—until he was bitten on the face—but had never been much of an outdoorsy kid. When he was in high school, his father took him into the mountains to hunt just once. "It was a disaster," Mamoru says. "I borrowed my mother's gun but I couldn't really shoot it. I just wasn't good at those sorts of things. And my father never asked me to come along again."

When he was nineteen, in the fall of 1972, Mamoru announced that he wanted to go to New York City "to study." He thought he might learn French so he could wind up in Paris, or that he might study photography or design. A hush fell over house. Since when did Mamoru care about studying anything? "He always had lots of confidence," Morie says, "and did whatever he wanted. He was very hard to control." Still, Morie continued to try. He told Mamoru that he could leave for America with his parents' blessing if he spent one winter on the top of the mountain working for the local mushroom farmer.

Mushroom farming was considered a lowly job, possibly the

lowest kind of farming there was. It wasn't thought to require much skill or intelligence. The farmhand's job consisted of collecting *nameko*, or sticky mushrooms, that grew on the roots of trees in the late fall, and then drying them in the sunshine every day, bringing them inside at night and before a snowfall. Without electricity or running water, the assistant mushroom farmers lived in unheated shacks and log cabins.

"It was a test," Mamoru says. "We all knew that. My dad thought I wouldn't be able to hack it—that I'd give up. That my arms would get tired from picking mushrooms and I'd come straight home."

He went up the mountain in November, before the snows came. His first task was to chop and split all the firewood for the winter, and after weeks of that, he could begin collecting the sticky mushrooms. They were soft, almost gelatinous, with a rich earthy aroma. He spent most of December picking them, eight to ten hours a day, and carrying them up a steep hill into the farmhouse about one half kilometer away.

The mushroom farmer was a friend of Uesugi's, and nice enough, but he drank enormous quantities of sake, even more than Morie, and tended toward long-winded stories of his hunting exploits. His wife was disfigured by a severe harelip and she was difficult to understand. While the other farmworkers lived in uncomfortable conditions—jammed into one small windowless room where they slept on straw mats—Mamoru was treated "like an honored guest, because I was the son of Kitako and Morie," he says. He was given a futon to sleep on in a "nice room on the first floor where the sun came in the windows." By the time he awoke in the morning, all the other farmhands were already dressed, out the door, and working.

From late December to the beginning of March, though, it became more complicated on the top of the mountain due to the uninterrupted tedium. The snow was beautiful and deep, Mamoru says, "a dry, crisp, powdery snow," and the farmer let him soak in the farmhouse tub at night, but otherwise, "I just watched the mushrooms dry," Mamoru says. "I took them outside in the morning to sit in the sunshine, and then brought them inside at night." After dinner, there was nothing to do but "listen to the mushroom farmer tell his hunting and pioneering stories, or listen to his harelip wife. We drank a lot. We ate good rice—really, the best rice you can get—and good miso. The vegetables had been kept fresh in snow under the kitchen floor. We had fish from the river, and unlimited mushrooms, of course. It was like being an Eskimo."

In the morning, when Mamoru was awakened by his own throbbing hangover, he'd find an inch of dry snow—"like crystal powder"—on the covers of his futon. The snow was so fine, and came down so relentlessly, that even the door and roof and window glass couldn't keep it out. It blew in like sand or dust.

"I made it through the winter though," Mamoru says, "and that surprised everybody, including myself. Actually, it was an incredible experience." At the beginning of March, he came down from the mountain and immediately made plans to leave for America.

He promised Yumi that he'd write and urged her to visit him during college vacations. Kitako sent him off with the Bible that her grandmother had left her—an American church member had signed it. As promised, Morie gave his blessing to his son, but offered no money. The mushroom farmer appeared, out of the blue, and gave Mamoru part of the proceeds from mushroom sales—one thousand dollars—but it was hardly enough to begin a new life in New York. In a desperate attempt to raise funds at the last minute, Mamoru told his father that he was going to visit his old high school principal on the way to Tokyo, and wanted to take him a puppy as a gift. He took the puppy to Tokyo instead and sold it for three hundred dollars. "I got myself a plane ticket and a three-piece suit," he says. "I have a feeling it might have been one of Happiness's puppies too."

He flew to New York City on March 19, 1973, his twenty-third birthday. It was the first time he had been on a plane. "Because it was my birthday," he says, "I was invited into the cockpit and the pilot signed my passport." He wouldn't return to the mountains for a long time. There were immigration issues, and in those early years, money issues, but even after he landed a job as a hairstylist at Vidal Sassoon in New York—the hippest international salon of that era— and returned to Tokyo as something of a celebrity, he didn't go back to Kurikoma to visit his parents until 1979. Bad memories kept him away, and lingering resentments. But also, he was living a fast-paced life by then—nights of drugs and dancing at Studio 54, and so many one-night affairs that he can't remember all the different women ("and maybe they don't remember me either," he says). The mountains seemed to offer nothing.

Every year for the New Year holidays, though, Kitako received glamorous gifts from her youngest son. There were scarves from Pucci and Hermès, and cashmere sweaters from Pringle. She wore them on special occasions but otherwise kept them neatly folded in tissue, stored together at the bottom of her nicest trunk. When she heard that Mamoru had been in Japan and hadn't come to see her, Kitako never mentioned it to him. He was young and busy, she told herself. And of all her children, he seemed to be having the life she had always wanted.

KITAKO WASN'T INTERESTED in bear hunting. Killing rabbits was enough. She couldn't help but notice that while Morie claimed he took "no pleasure in killing," when he and his hunting buddies came home after a bear hunt, they were loud, acted cocky—and took photographs of each other with their kill.

By the early 1970s, Uesugi was getting on in years. He was fit and ruggedly handsome, but nearly as old as the century. He talked about his age without embarrassment or even wistfulness, and wondered aloud whether he should start coloring his hair. Lots of old men in Japan were darkening their hair, he had noticed. Morie used to joke that he didn't have to worry about such things, since he barely had any hair left. But Morie did consider that Uesugi might have started teaching him how to hunt bear as a way to pass along the ways of the *matagi*. Uesugi's own son hadn't wanted to be one. And Uesugi worried that one day there wouldn't be any *matagi* left.

Over the years, as an informal apprentice to Uesugi, Morie had become locally famous as a bear hunter—and so adept at tracking bears in the mountains that the Kurikoma forestry office had awarded him a special year-round hunting permit "for the removal of dangerous animals." By the beginning of 1974, the year that Morie was ready to retire from Mitsubishi, he and Samurai Tiger had cornered ten bears together. Morie liked to give credit to his dog. Samurai Tiger was unflagging in his pursuit of bears. Once, when the dog had gotten the scent of a bear in the deep woods, he disappeared into the wild to track it on his own for three days—until Morie finally caught up with him.

At the end of 1974, just before the New Year holidays, Uesugi dropped by the house one night to report that a large bear had been spotted on the other side of the Mount Kurikoma peak. The heavy snows would begin, and the bear would settle into a cave for the winter; if they didn't find him soon, they'd have to wait until spring. A few nights later, Uesugi returned with his camping pack and stayed

Morie and his catch, a black Yezo bear, in 1973

over. In the early morning, he and Morie were joined by Den Naka-gawa, a local hunter and sharpshooter, and the three of them hiked up to the peak of Mount Kurikoma and made camp.

The next morning, Uesugi spotted some tracks and bear dung, so Morie let Samurai Tiger go ahead and the three men followed after him. The dog was hard to hold back. The minute he'd gotten the scent of the bear, he took off, his fur standing on end, his nose to the ground. "He had a one-track mind," Morie says, "and wasn't inter-ested in anything but finding that bear."

The three men followed the dog, making their way down the other side of the mountain. At a winter hot spring called Yubama, where long ago somebody had built a log cabin for bathers, the men caught up with Samurai Tiger. He'd tracked a large black bear with a white crescent on its throat—a Moon Bear—and had it cornered against the side of a rock ledge about fifty feet above them. The bear was growling, agitated, and swiping the air with its claws. Samurai Tiger was circling him, and kept spinning around, and after ten min-utes of this, the dog seemed to grow tired. Morie saw an opportunity to raise his shotgun and fire. The bullet went into the bear's ribs, as Morie had planned, but instead of dropping dead, the bear started screaming, and moving frantically, violently. A wounded bear has lots of tricks, as Morie knew, but Samurai Tiger grew bolder. Push-ing off with his strong back legs, he made several high lunges for the bear. And as Morie approached him, the dog became more deter-mined to succeed, lunging as high as he could. He was swiped on the head by a claw, and swiped again. It was against Uesugi's rule of only one bullet, but another shot was fired. Samurai Tiger slipped on the ledge of the rock wall and fell. "It was a long fall," Morie says, "and he landed on his head."

Uesugi and Nakagawa ran up the cliff and approached the bear. Its paws were still and open—a sure sign it was dead. Uesugi rolled the bear over and then, with Nakagawa, picked up the body, struggling a bit until they found a way to carry it down the steep hillside.

Below them, Morie crouched over Samurai Tiger, who was too weak to move. Morie picked up the dog and carefully balanced him over his shoulder, and then headed straight home. With the dog on his back, he hiked over the top of the mountain and back down again. It took most of the day.

Kitako remembers the three men arriving at the house about the same time, very late at night. Uesugi and Nakagawa had the bear. Its arms were tied to a pole. Morie held Samurai Tiger. "I felt so confused, so shocked," Kitako says. "I couldn't imagine what to do." The men looked dazed—their faces seemed strange. Uesugi put the bear down. Morie put Samurai Tiger in his kennel next to the house.

Kitako looked around. "There was the bear. There was our dog. Two big animals—one is dead, one is dying—and I felt very sad," she says. The men had peeled off their hunting clothes and were drinking, raising glasses of sake and toasting Samurai Tiger. They relived their bear hunt story, puffed up with bravado. Hunting talk. Man talk. Cold-hearted talk—no feeling. Kitako wondered who had been brave but the dog. Out in his kennel, Samurai Tiger was on his side, not moving much. Had he been hit by a bullet? Whose? From what Kitako had seen, the injury was more than just a head wound. But nobody was saying. Nobody would ever say. Inside the house, the men moved from hunting stories to war tales. Something about the day had taken them back, far back, to awful experiences, to other moments of chaos and confusion and danger and split-second decisions they'd have to live with forever. They'd moved from mountain talk to battle talk, and it wasn't bears anymore, but men, other men, enemies, friends, fellow soldiers they'd seen hunted down and killed in terrible ways, as if trying to calm themselves with worse comparisons.

The next morning, Wataru came to the house. "Such a great dog," he said. "Let's drink and celebrate Samurai Tiger all day." Sake was poured, more toasts to Samurai Tiger rose up, and cheers. Morie described again how fearless the dog was—to face an enemy as mean and strong as a Moon Bear. "I've never seen a better dog, a more courageous dog," Uesugi said. Wataru kept walking to the sake closet and getting another bottle, and soon there was a line of empty ones.

Nobody seemed eager to see the dog, or touch him. He was injured and possibly dangerous. That's how it seemed. So it was left to Kitako. She went outside alone, quietly, without saying anything, and rinsed the matted blood and dirt from his fur with cold water. Samurai Tiger's eyes followed hers, but he remained still. She made a paste of yellow sulfur powder—dried mud from the hot springs—and gently pressed it into the dog's wounds. He drank water from her cupped hand. And he began to eat. But he couldn't get up from his side. That's how he stayed for a couple of weeks. Weak, barely there, but eating.

Morie did not believe in putting a dog down. All his dogs lived their natural lifespan until, as he put it, "the day they were meant to die." It took Tiger almost a month. He fought hard that way too. "On his last day, he had only water and soup," Kitako says. "He was very quiet and weak, just trying to open his eyes. He wasn't suffering and didn't seem in pain. There was only sadness—ours."

At sunrise the next morning, Morie went outside. He was always up at dawn—doing stretches and judo exercises, and checking on the dogs before walking them. Kitako heard the sounds of his wailing from inside the house. She followed the noise to Tiger's kennel, where she found Morie on the ground with the dog in his arms. "We cried and we cried," Kitako says, "both of us, all day. Together."

Morie dug the grave, one and a half meters deep. And he carved a wooden marker. The funeral was even more elaborate, and bigger, than the one for Victory Princess a few years before: a black funeral car, a Shinto priest, a crowd of mourners, a solemn feast followed by more lively toasts and remembrances. Uesugi was there, and Nakagawa and his son. Wataru and Masutaro Ito. Mamoru was in New York but remembers hearing about it on the phone. "It was like a person had died."

The bear was skinned. Morie and Uesugi donated the massive pelt to the Akita Preservation Museum in Odate where it can be seen to this day, hanging on a wall. Morie still has the bullet that killed the bear—it flattened where the soft lead hit bone—and he keeps it in the same closet as Samurai Tiger's thick pelt, which is rolled along with the pelts of Three Good Lucks, Homan, and Victory Princess. "I touch the pelt," Morie says, "and I remember everything."

Eight

Shiro

Shiro was a fat fuzzy white puppy who turned into a leggy, elegant snowdrift—and champion—by the time he was one year old. Morie had been raising Akitas in the north for forty-five years by then and he felt he was "starting to get the hang of things." It didn't hurt that he'd known the dog's parents, grandparents, great-grandparents, great-great-grandparents . . . Actually, he'd known every single ancestor that had been involved in the creation of Shiro going back twenty years.

And by the time Shiro had won every award that an Akita could win in the snow country, Morie and his dogs were legendary. Dog enthusiasts came to see them and photograph them. Newspapers and magazines published stories about them. Television crews turned up with snaking cables and long lenses. Morie was embarrassed by the attention but it wouldn't be true to say he didn't like it.

He had more time on his hands after he finally retired from Mitsubishi in 1975, and he gave the dogs as much of himself, and as much of the wild, as he could. He fussed over Shiro and his other dogs, discussing them with Kitako and Wataru and a network of doddering old dog buddies who still appeared at the house for the vital mix of dog talk and sake. No matter how many years would pass, Morie got anxious when a new litter was about to be born. There was always the chance that another Samurai Tiger might appear. "They say you get only one dog like him in your lifetime," Morie says, "but I thought if I lived long enough, I might get two, and prove that saying wrong."

HIS RETIREMENT CAME AT the perfect moment. Each of the power plants he'd built was still operating smoothly, efficiently, and the improvements he'd made over the decades had made him almost obsolete. Right after World War II, it had cost seventeen yen to produce one kilowatt-hour of energy at a power plant in the snow country. By the time Morie retired, one kilowatt-hour cost only two yen. And while it had required sixteen workers to keep the Kurikoma plant operating in the late 1960s, now the plant ran virtually by itself. All of them did. When Morie made rounds and oversaw his final inspection, it was like visiting one ghost ship after another.

He was fifty-nine when he left Mitsubishi and he assumed he wouldn't live much longer—maybe another decade at the most. His four older brothers were already dead, from too little exercise and too much sake, and by 1975, the friend he cared most about in life, Uesugi, was beginning to show his age. The *matagi* had hired an assistant to accompany him on bear hunts, when he had farther to travel, or had heavier loads to carry. He needed help hacking through the dense forest, too. Before a long hunting trip, Uesugi had started dropping by the house of one of his wives, a hairdresser, to have his hair and mustache trimmed and dyed darker, his fingernails cleaned and filed, his feet scrubbed and his toenails clipped. He confessed to Kitako that if he died while hunting—which is how he hoped to go—he wanted to leave a clean and handsome body behind in the forest. He prayed to the mountain god before every hunting trip, too, asking for an auspicious death in the wild. Morie dreaded the day.

As much as Morie had spent his years as a husband suppressing Kitako's independence, and his time as a father pushing his children out of the nest, he found that as retirement approached, the entire family—even his children who lived in other countries and rarely saw him—had a great deal to say about what he should do.

"People had lots of ideas and suggestions about where I should retire," Morie says, "including my children. So I checked out all kinds of places, and really made a study . . . We traveled all over, looking at so many different towns and cities. There was one spot we liked, where the emperor has a summer home, but it wasn't wild enough for me."

Kitako made no secret of her desire to return to Tokyo, or even the outskirts of Tokyo, but the economy was soaring in those boom years and everybody in Japan suddenly seemed rich, or richer. Kitako's sisters and their families had second homes and boats and Western designer clothes. They traveled and collected photograph albums full of snapshots of Paris and London, or pictures of themselves in New York City with Mamoru. But living in the snow country, working as a power plant chief and raising dogs, hadn't made Morie rich by any measure. His pension was hardly enough to buy a small house in Sendai.

There were lots of pretty spots in the north, larger towns and cities near rural areas where Morie could run the dogs—Kitako was open to this compromise—but Morie didn't like the way they had been developed. The houses all looked the same to him, and they sat so close to each other. "Living in remote areas so much of my life had spoiled me," he says. And he couldn't help but notice how unhealthy urban people looked. "They didn't look like they were getting any real exercise—or fresh air," he says. "And their dogs looked worse." One of the big breeders in Odate admitted that he exercised his Akitas while driving alongside them on a motorbike. Another dog buddy had invented something even easier: He jammed the dog leashes in the door of his van and drove around the block, over and over.

Investigating the development plans for some quieter towns in the snow country, Morie obtained government studies and internal Mitsubishi documents and discovered that in several places the ground water had been polluted by mining. He'd remembered that when he traveled with his dogs to some of these places, they had refused to drink the water, even when it bubbled up from an underground spring.

As he traveled throughout the north and imagined where he and Kitako might wind up, Morie was always running into people he knew, old neighbors, old dog buddies, or friends of friends dating back decades. Sometimes, he'd introduce himself and find that his reputation preceded him. People seemed to recollect how he had brought electricity to their town, or raised fine dogs, or showed movies in his house in the years right after the war—or they had heard about his amazing electric bathtub. On a trip to Shimizu, when Morie and Kitako went to see their old friend Masutaro Ito, the local farmers greeted them like visiting royalty. "The red carpet was really rolled out," Kitako says. "Everybody was so grateful to us for giving them Hoko. I think that's the very first time I said to myself, maybe this nice reward is better than if we'd sold all those dogs for money."

While hunting in the foothills of Mount Kurikoma one morning with Uesugi, Morie found himself on a beautiful slope of land over-

looking the reservoir of the Kurikoma dam. It was a serene spot—
and felt somehow enchanted—that abutted a protected forest on
three sides. Warm and verdant, the land was on the south side of the
mountain, where it was sheltered from the north wind and the
fiercest winter storms, and also where the sun lingered all afternoon.
Uesugi reminded Morie that they both knew the owner of the land.
He might be persuaded to sell.

Morie was struck by the unique situation—a rare slice of land in a
national forest. There was even an *onsen* nearby, and the mountains
that he and Kitako both loved. He laughed that he hadn't thought of it
before: Kurikoma had splendid weather, milder than Akita, its meadows and forests were pristine and exquisite, the water was clear and
clean. If he remained there, Morie could keep his special hunting permit that allowed him to travel the forests year-round, the way Uesugi
did, and his dogs could have almost unlimited room to run. "Suddenly," Morie says, "I realized that I was already living in the best
place of all."

When Morie dropped by to see the owner of the property, the
man came to the entrance of his house to greet him and said, "I knew
you'd wind up here."

A deal was struck almost immediately. Morie was too overwhelmed with excitement to bother with extended negotiations. The
land was expensive, and there wouldn't be much money left to build
a house, but look what he'd own! There was four thousand *tsubo* of
land, more than three acres, and best of all: "You couldn't see a soul,
or another house, from any part of the property," Morie says. "It
was almost unthinkable in Japan."

Kitako might even be proud of him for finding such an idyllic
spot, he thought. As soon as she had started hunting, she'd changed—
grown happier and more engaged, almost as gleeful as Morie was

about mountain life. She was keeping a journal of wildflowers and mountain plants, trying to learn the names of everything. She asked her sisters to send a set of botanical encyclopedias. She began to study ikebana, or flower arranging, and foraged on the hillsides with garden clippers in her hand in search of beautiful wildflowers. Surely her dreams of living in Tokyo were silly and obsolete, and just something she clung to out of habit. Besides, the *Shinkansen* bullet train would be extended to the north in the next few years, with stops nearby in Sendai and Ichinoseki. Morie knew people on the *Shinkansen* planning board and wondered if he might be able to have some sway. A train stop in Kurikoma would make Kitako happy, wouldn't it? She'd be over the moon.

But Morie had guessed wrong. Rather than being thrilled by his purchase of the land, Kitako and the rest of the family was appalled that he had gone ahead and made his own retirement decision without consulting them. As for the bullet train coming to Kurikoma: Certainly this would never come true.

Thinking that if she saw the spectacular land, Kitako would soften her view, Morie took her to the hillside that he'd bought with almost all of their nest egg. As Kitako would relate later to her children on the phone, Morie drove as far as he could to access the land, then parked by the side of the road and led her on foot almost a mile in the wilderness, through thorns and dense groves of bamboo, to see the hillside property. It was in the middle of nowhere. Had he lost his mind? "I felt very bad for my mother," Ryoko says, "and I didn't know what to say."

"When I heard about the land, I couldn't believe it," Mamoru says. "I thought maybe all that sake had gone to his brain."

Morie spent weeks trying to explain: "We have the best dogs, best rice, best water, best sake—right here in Kurikoma—and next, the

Shinkansen will be coming right to our door. You'll see. This will be the best place in all Japan."

Night after night, Kitako was too upset to talk. In her futon on the floor, she rolled over and faced the sliding shoji screen instead of Morie. After years of waiting for her turn, she discovered she wouldn't get one. After years of dreaming about living in the city again, near coffee shops and restaurants with foreign food, near taxis and buses, she was going to wind up on a piece of land that was a mile from any road and inaccessible by car or tractor. Living with Morie and his dogs for decades had been bad enough, but now, to wind up in a place of boulders and bamboo was too much. Worse yet, there was hardly any money to build a decent house.

"We had many loud fights, many disagreements," says Kitako. "We argued about it for weeks, months. Eventually he said he understood that what he'd done was unfair. And he understood if I had to leave. 'Go if you want,' he said to me. 'You are free to go.'"

MORIE DIDN'T KNOW what he was thinking when he asked a city girl to marry him. It was hard to fathom how different their expectations of life could be. Things like this were impossible to see or understand when you met someone. Maybe his judgment had been skewed by the war. The war colored everything, and darkened everything, forced your mind to play tricks. It distracted you with unpleasant images and memories and made you forget the things you needed to remember most.

War? He'll show you his diaries, date books, his assignment papers—he's kept everything from his seven years of service, but these days Morie doesn't want to talk about it much, except to say that while he saw many countrymen die on the fronts in China—Nanjing and Shanghai—he never heard one Japanese soldier cry out, *Tennoheika Banzai!*, in praise of the emperor at their moment of death, the way they'd been trained to do.

"They'd say *Mother!* as they died, or they'd call out the name of a child," Morie says. "That's what I learned. No matter how patriotic and loyal you are, when you are dying, you express something from the deepest part of you—and call out to what you love most."

What did he love most? He was so homesick in the navy that he dreamt about the mountains nearly every night. He missed the austere winter, craved the whiteness, and the cold, and the way the sloped roofs of the snow country houses looked against a snowy hillside. He thought about the sheets of ice over the lake, over the creeks, and the foggy frozen puddles. Sometimes in his dreams he was a boy again, making a pair of skis from two grave markers he'd stolen from the village cemetery. The wooden markers were tall and narrow, and Morie could shave them down, shape them, and make perfect cross-country skis.

On shore leave, if he had tried to go to Castle No. 5 Town, he would have spent the entire time on the train—it was twenty-four hours each way—so he went to Tokyo instead. At the house of his academy roommate, Kato, he met a girl, his roommate's younger sister. For the duration of several visits, she didn't have a name. She was a vibrancy, a spirit, that he could sense when she entered the room. When he paid closer attention to her, Morie noticed she had thick wavy hair, small round spectacles, a sharp look in her eyes—a kind of clarity and strength that he liked. She was smart, Morie could see that immediately. And she wasn't afraid of him.

Back on duty, on a minesweeper near the Shanghai front in China, Morie's ship patrolled the Yangtze River searching for and dismantling explosive mines. One night, after a string of dull days with nothing happening, there was a great explosion—the ship hit a floating mine, blowing the stern of the sweeper, all its pieces and men, through the air. Morie was asleep one moment and in the water the next, swimming as fast as he could from the burning ship. He reached for a piece of wood, a plank or bench seat, flotsam, and held on. There were bodies of other men in the water, bobbing in the dark current, facedown, lifeless, and others were calling out, or crying. Swept up in the black water and its swirling current, Morie drifted away, lost on the river.

Morning came. The first light of dawn. He was still drifting. The river had turned pale yellow-green. Following the current, he was getting closer to the front, rather than farther from it, and Morie wondered if he'd start passing enemy boats or men on the shore with guns. He was a strong swimmer—having spent every summer at Lake Hachiro near his village—and felt lucky for that.

Something moved in the water near him. It was a dark, shiny shape, a dolphin—sleek and finless. There were two dolphins, and then more. They were river dolphins, a whole school of them, rolling over in the water, spinning around. They swam silently, diving gently, playing softly with each other. Morie kept waiting for them to swim off, or turn around, but they bobbed and shimmied and floated alongside him, watching him, and playing, hour after hour. They studied him. They stayed with him. It was as though they'd decided to make him their leader, or mascot, or a god they were worshipping. Their companionship felt magical. It was almost a vigil. And by the end of the first day, they seemed like the best friends he'd ever had in life.

A patrol boat spotted Morie on his third night—flashed its lights and came after him. He was so weak, he had to be helped up the ladder. And when he stood on deck and looked back to the river, the dolphins were gone.

Fifty-eight men had been blown overboard, he was told. Morie was one of five who had survived.

What did Morie love most? He was discharged from the Imperial Navy with medals and ribbons and letters of recommendation for jobs in Tokyo, and he roamed the bars of Ginza and Yokohama night after night. He just wanted to have fun. "There was no talk of love during the war," he says. "I only wanted to drink." He returned to Castle No. 5 Town a decorated hero, and was much admired by his younger sisters and the old men in the village who clustered around him, nodding encouragingly—but there was nothing for Morie in Castle No. 5 Town except approval. There was no job, no house, no prospects of any kind. Everybody told him to go to Tokyo. That's where all the smart engineers found jobs, made money, and got rich. That's where anybody talented would wind up. While interviewing for various positions, again he stayed at the Katos' house in Azabu.

Kitako. That was her name.

The family seemed to push Morie toward her. There wasn't any arm-twisting or direct words—only whispers, subtle suggestions, a gentle force, like the wind or gravity, that brought them into the same room or seated them next to each other at meals and family gatherings. In those days, a man was supposed to marry. There was a time frame for everything, a sense of inevitability. One thing led to another. School, job, marriage. Families conspired to make things happen. It was something society wanted for you, wanted for everybody. To Morie, their marriage felt arranged. Kitako would always insist that it was not.

She was gregarious and friendly, and seemed to know what Morie was thinking. She always said "good morning" with such vigor, like she meant it, like her day was being made by the very sight of him. She was hardworking, too, despite the fancy Azabu address. That

Kitako on her nineteenth birthday

made him respect her. She worked as a typist for a large corporation, but had earned a teaching degree too. At nineteen, she was making more money than Morie was.

Love? It seemed more like mutual respect. It was a certain kind of intelligence meeting another kind of intelligence. Later on, he had a crush on her—when they were first married, and living in Manchuria in 1940—and afterward, something else took its place, something more complicated and impossible to talk about because there weren't words. "Nobody talked about love," Morie says. The Kato family seemed happy about the match. Mr. Kato was a successful barber and went into the fine houses and corporate offices to cut the hair of some of the richest and most influential men in Tokyo. He was a gentleman with refined, good manners. But he had six daughters, after all, and somebody had to marry them.

THERE WERE SO MANY RESTRICTIONS that came with building a house in a national park, or next to one, Morie sometimes wondered if he'd ever live on the land, or ever stop filing for permits. Only certain trees could be cut, but for every single tree cut, another tree had to be planted, and a separate permit was needed for each. Other trees couldn't be cut or pruned—only transplanted. There were other spots on the property, at the edge of the forest, where the foliage and plant life couldn't be touched at all.

Morie picked the site for the house. He designed the slope and curve of the driveway. He saw it perfectly in his mind's eye and drew his plans on paper. The house would be hidden from the road, but would have a view of the reservoir, a ridge of mountains, and the open sky. He designed a cistern where the spring water would collect and run into the house. He began clearing for the driveway, chopping down dense groves of bamboo with an axe and saw and digging up the boulders when he came to them. But in the stretch of driveway, about one hundred meters long, there were dozens of boulders so massive that he couldn't lift them alone.

When his shovel hit a rock that was too heavy to pry up and roll away by himself, Morie would dig a hole right next to it—a hole that was much deeper and bigger than the boulder itself.

And then he'd call out.

"*K'a-san!*—Momma!"

It was Kitako's job to help with the largest boulders. She would take a long, thick bar of steel and wedge it underneath the rock as a lever. When Morie was done digging, he came around to her side and together they pried up the boulder and dropped it into the hole that he had just dug.

"Then we covered it with dirt," Kitako says. "Think of how the pyramids were made, and you get the idea. But there were hundreds of Egyptians and usually only two of us."

Kitako was born in the year of the dog. Maybe that's why she stayed, she says. A dog never tells you it's staying, it just does.

The house was small, and simple, two stories and six rooms—a long central hallway, several tatami rooms, a dining room and kitchen. It would have a red sloping metal roof, a root cellar, and a place for Morie's electric bathtub. Even so, when Morie heard how much it would cost to build, he found wood from an old dormitory nearby to reuse. And he told the contractor: "It only has to last ten years. When I die, my wife will be moving to Tokyo."

They moved in slowly, making two dozen trips to the house with their belongings loaded into the back of their old Toyota Corolla van. There were snowshoes, skis, winter clothes, old trunks, scrolls,

Morie and Kitako's house being built, 1975

books, dog trophies, two unusual tree stumps that had been made into side tables. Over the years, they'd collected quite a few mountain souvenirs, most of them gifts from Uesugi: the shell of a giant sea turtle, a huge empty wasp's nest, an enormous white swan that Uesugi said he found dead by the side of a lake and had stuffed.

Morie and Kitako wanted to have a view of the reservoir from their second-floor bedroom, but not an unobstructed view, which they felt would be boring. So they left a rare old tree at the center of the property, a gnarled pine that rose up between the house and the dam. "Our neighbors kept telling us to cut it down," Morie says. "That it was ugly and old and ruining our view. But Kitako and I both liked it. We thought it looked old and important."

The rest of the garden was truly a collaborative effort. Friends from all over the north arrived with trees and shrubs and perennials for Morie and Kitako to plant. They came with cherry trees and plum trees, cypresses and cedars and oaks, both saplings and fresh cuttings. Uesugi brought treasure after treasure, including rare rhododendrons that he'd pulled up from the deepest part of the Kurikoma forest. Morie began creating a bank of azaleas and rhododendrons below the house, a hedge that would bloom throughout the month of May. He had a dream that in springtime, looking out from their bedroom, he and Kitako would enjoy the clouds of brilliant color below them and a gorgeous view of the reservoir and green mountains beyond.

Over the years, Morie worked very hard on the garden—spending as much time as he spent with the dogs—and found his efforts profoundly rewarding. "There are few things," he says, "that make me as happy as planting a tree." Eventually, there would be more than one hundred different kinds of mountain flowers, and two hundred and fifty varieties of azalea and rhododendron.

He and Kitako quarreled most in the spring and fall, when Morie

Winter view from the house

pruned the garden. "Kitako always had an opinion," Morie says. "She also complains about the placement of stones, but after a certain point, it was hard to move them. . . .

"She and I have always fought a lot. We really have it out. We say exactly what we think. And there are lots of things we don't agree on. But we can always have a good fight. That's the strength of our marriage."

THE COMING YEARS brought many changes, and losses, but Morie and Kitako endured. In 1979, Mamoru returned to the snow country for the first time since moving to America, and on the long train ride from Tokyo, he had mixed feelings. He couldn't believe what a no-man's-land Kurikoma seemed, so remote, so slow, but he was surprised when he reached the house to see how tranquil things were between his parents, and how comfortable their life was. The house was simple and perfect, the garden like a sanctuary.

He was curious about how Yumi Sato was doing. She had written letters from medical school to Mamoru, but mostly talked about how much studying she had to do. Her letters had stopped three or four years before. Mamoru had gotten busy too, and was preoccupied with his new life. The small world of Yumi and the Satos had slipped so far away from the salon of Vidal Sassoon where Mamoru spent his days, and Studio 54, where he spent his nights.

"Yumi died," Atsuko told him. "She died last year."

Mamoru went to the Satos' house in Masaka to express his sympathy and was told that Yumi had fought brain cancer for several years before dying—something she had never mentioned in her letters. Dr. and Mrs. Sato took him into Yumi's bedroom, which they'd preserved exactly as it had been when Yumi was a teenager. They gave Mamoru all her record albums and in a bag made of beautiful fabric, they gave him the letters that their daughter had written to him over the last three years as she struggled with cancer. "I'm going to stop the treatment," she wrote in several of them, "and run away to see you." They were addressed, stamped, but never posted.

The following year, 1980, Dr. Sato died and his hospital was sold. Mrs. Sato returned to Tokyo. Without a job as an X-ray technician, Wataru Ito came to live full-time with Morie and Kitako, earning his keep by doing odd jobs and chores.

The same year, Uesugi gave up his position as inspector of the Kurikoma forest—and his permit to hunt year-round. He moved in with his last wife, a younger woman, in Ichinoseki, and led a quieter life. As a *matagi*, he had killed seventy bears by himself, and dozens more with the aid of partners. He used to laugh that he'd made twenty million yen over his lifetime in bears, and he'd used the money to put his nine children through school. He was proud that two of them had graduated from college. Uesugi cared about education, he told Kitako, because he himself had never learned to read or write.

He would live another sixteen years. He died at ninety-four in 1996—at home, not in the mountains, as he had once wished—with a full head of hair and a lot of grandchildren, none of whom were interested in becoming a *matagi*. Morie had been Uesugi's only student. At the time of his death, there weren't any Moon Bears left to hunt anyway. And any surviving *matagi* was a living relic. Uesugi lived long enough to have books written about him, and a television special. He brought a bear's dried gall bladder to the television station and a dead poisonous snake in a bag. He demonstrated how to extract venom from a snake by squeezing its head. During the on-camera interviews,

Uesugi's grave and scotch at Ganjo-ji

Uesugi's old-style Akita accent was so strong and his choice of words so colloquial, subtitles in standard Japanese were needed.

After his death, Uesugi's wife gave his *matagi* hunting license, an ancient scroll that had been passed down to him, to the Iwate prefecture museum, along with his ivory hunting club, his hunting knife, his handmade snowshoes, his collection of bear skulls, and his carved wooden sculpture of the mountain god. He was buried at Ganjo-ji, a twelve-hundred-year-old Buddhist temple in Ichinoseki, under an old bronze Shakyamuni Buddha. In the fall of 2006, Mamoru and his brother-in-law Noritsugu visited the temple and left Uesugi a bottle of single-malt scotch.

"Uesugi was an exceptional person and we could talk all week about him," Morie says. "Charming, wild, strong. He was really the human embodiment of all the traits that I was trying to breed in my dogs."

As the years passed, Morie and Kitako's mountain life grew a bit noisier and faster. In Kurikoma, roads were built, and then widened. Their driveway no longer descended to meet a snaking dirt road, but a highway. A new station for the bullet train opened to great excitement in 1990—some of the strings Morie had pulled and arms he had twisted may have done some good. And it turned out that Kitako didn't have to go to Tokyo to see her children and growing brood of grandchildren. They all wanted to come to the mountains. Morie had a guesthouse built on the property so they would stay as long as they liked. The bullet train brought other people too—hikers, tourists, developers of ski resorts, and there was more traffic around the dam and reservoir. Compared to the congested cities and other parts of Japan, Kurikoma remained sleepy and tranquil and unpolluted. In fact, the mountain spring was so pure, a company came to bottle and sell the water.

In 1989, when Morie turned seventy-five, he decided to reduce his consumption of sake to one glass a day. It wouldn't be so terrible to live a bit longer. It was so agreeable in Kurikoma, and the garden was beautiful, and the hiking and hunting were as wonderful and challenging as ever. He ordered a new snow-blowing machine for the winter. And he picked out a puppy that would be coming to live with them soon, too.

He drank the sake each night before dinner from a tall clear glass. The rice wine made his face turn red and his body warm. He savored every gulp, and felt, after all this time, that together with a soak in his electric tub, it was the finest way to get through the long cold country winter.

SHIRO ARRIVED THE YEAR AFTER the new bullet train station in Kurikoma opened. The station was spacious and modern, as if something from the distant future had been dropped down in the rice fields and green mountains. Shiro had a modern quality too. His face was delicate. His legs were improbably long. Even as a puppy, he had an air of world-weary bemusement that seemed both teenaged and aristocratic.

Since the 1980s, the dog world of the north had begun to favor an Akita with a slightly different look—longer and thinner legs, a more foxlike snout and triangular eyes—but by the early 1990s, this style of dog prevailed as the new standard in Japan. It had been a long, slow struggle since the end of World War II, when the dog men of the snow country had simply hoped to produce litters of puppies with erect ears and curling tails. Now the days of the hodgepodge dogs were over. The stout bodies, bear-shaped heads, and shepherd faces were gone, too. The traces of cross-breeding with Western dogs in the early part of the century had been erased. And when two of these Japanese Akitas were bred, there weren't surprises—but a perfectly uniform litter of dogs so similar it was nearly impossible to tell them apart.

The result was a smaller, more finely featured Akita than those in America and elsewhere. That didn't bother the snow country breeders. Since the Akita was their native dog, they felt they were allowed to set trends, rather than follow them. But it was this, along with a desire to resist being influenced by the international market, and the way Akitas looked in other countries, that led the Japan Kennel Club in 1996 to begin refusing to recognize Akitas from other countries, creating a split that has still not been reconciled. To many breeders and Akita clubs worldwide there are two distinct breeds, an "American" Akita and a Japanese one, something the American Kennel Club has not yet recognized.

Shiro was six years old when he entered the Hall of Fame and earned his place on the wall at the Akita Preservation Society Museum. Morie was proud to say that he wasn't just a show dog; he and Wataru still took him rabbit hunting. But in 1998, when Shiro was eight and Morie was eighty-two, they stopped hunting altogether. At the annual rabbit hunting event in November—the opening of hunting season when all the locals get together—Morie, as the second leader of the group, was charging up a mountain slope when he lost his footing. He stumbled on tree roots and fell on the ground. He was more embarrassed than hurt, but the fall jarred him. "That's when I realized that it was time to quit," he says. "A hunter has to be able to keep up with the leader or he should drop out. So I dropped out."

In 2000, Atsuko and her husband Noritsugu came to live in Kurikoma. After years of city life and long hours on the job, they thought they'd enjoy the mountains in their retirement and old age. Besides, Morie was eighty-four, and Kitako was eighty. Atsuko told her parents that she wanted to work on her cooking, and absorb some of her mother's lessons. Noritsugu wanted to become a vegetable gardener. "Don't expect to learn how to garden overnight," Morie told his son-in-law. "It'll take you ten years to be a decent farmer. And if you wait too long to begin, I'll be dead and won't be able to help you."

They moved into the second floor of the house, and moved Morie and Kitako into a downstairs bedroom, where it would be easier for them to get around. And after sixty years of cooking magnificently for her husband, and any visiting dog buddy or lost hiker who turned up at the door, Kitako retired from the kitchen. "I'm not as quick a cook as my mother," Atsuko says, "and it doesn't come as easily to me, but grocery shopping is certainly less difficult these days." She made friends with a local organic rice farmer who delivers an annual supply of rice to the house in the fall. She made friends with another local farmer who grows beans, cucumbers, radishes, carrots, and juicy hothouse tomatoes. For his part, Nori-chan, as the family still calls him, learned to plow the driveway in winter, harvest the vegetable garden in summer, and every fall and spring he receives lessons in pruning while Morie and Kitako stand nearby disagreeing about which limbs to cut. "The garden," Morie says, "is both a source of joy and many quarrels."

Shiro was twelve and Morie was eighty-eight when they were given lifetime achievement awards at a ceremony in Odate. Shiro became a national treasure. Morie was recognized for the contributions he had made to the traditional culture of Japan by raising native dogs. The emperor sent a letter. Television crews arrived. And so did the extended family. Atsuko and Noritsugu helped to host a large family celebration at the house. Ryoko, who was running a small animal hospital in Oyama City, came with her family. Moritake, who now owned and ran a Chinese restaurant in Yokohama, called with his congratulations. Mamoru arrived from New York—with a colorful entourage of glamorous friends in tow.

Only Wataru, the King of the Dog Boys, was missing. One day, during the winter of 2002, Morie was walking the dogs in the mountains and noticed red stains in the snow, which he identified as bloody urine. He realized it was the path where Wataru had been walking the dogs the evening before. "What's wrong with Wataru?" Morie had asked Kitako. She shook her head. "I think he's very sick." After forty years of being involved in every aspect of Morie's dog life, the King of the Dog Boys was sent back to his father's house in Shimizu, where he died six months later. Morie received the call on his birthday.

Without Wataru, it was hard to keep showing dogs. Shiro had collected every award in existence anyway. And where would Morie find the space to store any more trophies? It had taken Atsuko three months just to organize the dog stuff—the articles, leashes, medals, trophies, and the complete set of newsletters from the Akita Preservation Society going back to 1946. The only trophies Morie kept on display in the house were the old ones, the deep bronze drinking cups that Three Good Lucks won in the early fifties. "Those mean the most to me," he says.

In the old days, some of the trophies weren't that pretty, but they were solid metal, well made—and not too big. By 2003, the trophies were made from plastic, coated in gold and enormous. Morie wonders if these gilded trophies represent an unfortunate change of another kind. Slowly over the years as Japan became tamer and richer, he says, the Akitas changed too. Their faces are delicate and sweet. Their eyes are sensuous. Their mouths seem to curl up in a perpetual smile. They are cute dogs, happy dogs, pets—and nobody he knows hunts anymore. "In the rain sometimes you'll see owners carrying their dogs—not walking them to the car, but carrying them to protect them from the rain, the wet, the mud," Morie says. "It's to keep them looking pretty. You won't see me doing that."

He'd helped to preserve the Akita breed—the flesh and bones of the traditional snow country dog. But what about its heart and soul, its nature? The essence of the Akita—its unique spirit and ruggedness—now seemed unsuitable for the modern world. Could such traits survive in an environment that no longer required them or wanted them? "In the wild there is always a leader of an animal pack, the dominant dog that is chosen for its strength. But these days, there are fewer and fewer dogs that are true leaders because these aren't the dogs selected to be bred. It used to be that a leader was a dog that knew how to hunt. Now the dog that succeeds is a pet that simply exists to please its owner and receive affection."

If a dog wasn't intelligent, strong, and resourceful, couldn't survive in the mountains, sleep in the snow, corner bears and wild antelope, or save a life—would anyone but Morie care? "I worry that the dogs are losing their core aggressiveness and sharpness, their shrewdness," Morie says. "Having *kishō* means a fighting spirit. And I think it's a fighting spirit that has allowed the Akita to survive for centuries. But people want dogs to be useful to them, and so their traits are always desirable in relation to man, and what man wants from a dog."

Morie wondered where Japan was heading, where the world was heading, and where the dogs would wind up, if these animal instincts weren't honored and preserved. What will happen if the principles of nature—pure animal nature—got lost? When you rescued an animal from extinction, what was the most important thing to save, the body or the spirit? "Over the years, I was able to help contribute to the survival of the Akita, and contribute to their shape—how they looked—and their health," Morie says. "But I still wish that someone would help me to work on the instincts. I want to start to recover them."

Nine

Morie and Kitako

They live by the mountain clock. The summer is green and lush and hot. Fall comes early, with a chill in the afternoon, and the dogs run into the wild twice as fast. According to Morie, the foliage peaks on October 27, almost every year, and on November 3, there is a large regional dog show at the park in Odate. By then Kitako is pickling green apples that blew down in the autumn typhoons, and preserving daikon radish to eat over the winter. She makes wine from the fall grapes which the whole family will drink together on New Year's Day.

When Morie greets a dog or talks about a dog—or is remembering a dog he knew once—he becomes a different person. Not that he's walled off from other people. He can converse, and amuse, and make fun of himself. He can sit at the head of the dinner table and his voice rises to a yelp or lowers to a growl (this happens quite a lot), and he can tell a story that keeps everybody with him laughing. His grandchildren talk about him lovingly. His children do too, if pressed. And when lost hikers arrive at his door in the dark, asking for directions, they are frequently ushered inside, invited to the table for sake and some food, and sometimes to stay overnight in the guesthouse. At the holidays, his mailbox bursts with cards and greetings from well-wishers and former colleagues and the daughters and sons of old buddies now gone.

But when you ask him about the dogs, he changes—his voice softens, his smile goes from reluctant to open and unself-conscious. It goes from a social smile to a heartbreaking one. Morie can be imposing at times, and along with his size and strength (you should see his judo exercises), his vocalizing and samurai sound effects, he can be a little overbearing. But when the subject is dogs, his smile becomes gentle—guileless, shy—and reveals a hint of what lies beneath, as though there's a direct line from Morie's heart, or whatever you want to call where he's keeping his memories of all those dogs, to his smile. A current of calm, sweet energy.

THE AIR IS CLEAN and cool. The sunlight is sharp. The sky is glistening, blue and clear, shining over the park in Odate where the dog crowd—owners, handlers, dog boys, dog media—has gathered for the big show. It's May 3, 2006, and spring is peaking in the snow country. Everybody is picnicking on the grounds of the park, sitting on large blue blankets, leaning over tiny hibachi grills and colorful *bento* boxes of lunch, under clouds of pale pink cherry blossoms that are just beginning to drift to the ground.

Akita dogs are everywhere, sitting and sleeping and peering out of shadowy crates. They are walked on leashes, and some smaller ones—curly-tailed puppies—are lounging on their owners' laps. You see Akitas on the backs of T-shirts, on gold pins and rings, on belt buckles, bumper stickers, and vibrant green 2006 "Year of the Dog" calendars. Once in a while you'll see a few brown Akitas, or all-white ones like Shiro (which means "White" or, if you want to sweeten it, "Whitey"), but mostly the dogs at the show, and in the park, and even on the backs of windbreakers and T-shirts are pale reddish Akitas with white faces. "Every decade has its own look," Morie says, "and now everybody wants a red dog with a white face. In a few years, it'll be something else."

He and Kitako arrive in a new Toyota Land Cruiser driven by their granddaughter, Yukari, a tall, thin woman in her thirties with cascading hair and large eyes and two elegant brown Egyptian salukis in the back of the SUV. Salukis are ancient dogs—primitives like the Akita—but thin-coated, and as sleek and lean as Yukari. When she comes to Kurikoma to see her grandparents and parents, her dogs run all over the mountains, thrilled to have more wild space and clean air. At night, they are allowed in the house, wandering wherever they please and getting into trouble. Morie seems amused by this. And he seems delighted when Yukari's dogs beg for food at the table, or jump on him. It's hard to be the child of a dog nut like Morie, but still, something was passed down. One of his other granddaughters, Masako Ando, is a clinical veterinarian. And his daughter Ryoko keeps so many dogs at home—she runs an animal rescue shelter, as well as a small animal hospital in Oyama City— that her own children can't keep their names straight.

In Odate, the officials of the show catch sight of Morie and Kitako and greet them with deep bows, then usher them to a long table under an awning, a place of honor, where cups of green tea are served, and some kind of biscuit. Sitting there, watching the dog show as if it had been staged for their amusement and pleasure, Morie and Kitako look like royalty. They sit erect, formal. Morie wears a navy blue sweater, and a dark beret that he's been sporting to the shows for thirty years. His face is impassive as he stares out into the dog ring. ("None of the dogs today impressed me," he says later.) Kitako wears a pale gray wool sweater and thin wool scarf. She and Morie lightly make fun of each other, as they try to remember the names of the dog world representatives who drop by. Their faces are bright and receptive. The hands they hold out in greeting to old friends are smooth and unlined.

Kitako comes to the big shows, and has for decades now. She enjoys the lively crowds and the dog scene. These days she keeps a journal, writing down memories as they come to her. "When I read it over," she says, "I say to myself, I really survived something."

A few weeks earlier, Morie had given a speech in Sendai where he and Shiro were honored at a special exhibition. "I have no regrets," he told the crowd, and then he did something unprecedented: He thanked Kitako for her support and thanked his children for putting up with him. Usually, when Morie makes speeches, he's very traditional, reserved, and formal. Nothing personal is ever uttered. It was the first time he'd mentioned family members in a public way. And it was the first time he had ever spoken of Kitako in a speech. Word of it spread through the family like wildfire. *Did you hear? He mentioned her.*

"It made me very happy," says Atsuko.

"I think he's finally realizing," says Mamoru.

Kitako seems to have softened too. For years she wasn't sure why she married Morie, and wished she hadn't. Now she says she feels proud that she has spent her life with someone of such integrity and strength. "At least he has known what his life is about," she says. "So many times I wanted to run off. But now, after all these years, I find myself happy to be with such a man. I say this after a great deal of thought. I'm proud of his integrity, and that he's stuck to his beliefs all these years. He's really stood for something and that matters to me. Lately, I find myself full of energy and spirit to defend him."

View from under the awning, Odate, May 3, 2006

It's been sixty years since World War II ended and there were only a dozen or so Akitas left in Japan. Now they can be found in eighty-two countries on earth, and there are dozens of Akita clubs, breeders, and regional shows worldwide. There are between two and three thousand Akitas registered with the American Kennel Club in the United States alone, and hundreds of Japanese-style Akitas that aren't yet recognized by the AKC. Worldwide there are thousands more Akitas, according to the Fédération Cynologique Internationale (FCI). In Japan, where the younger generation seems to have moved on to other more exotic breeds, the number of members of the Akita Preservation Society has dropped in the last two decades. "Young people seem to have little interest in the Akita dog or showing them," says Koji Sasaki, the chairman of the Odate show. "In the old days, people were so competitive and emotional about Akitas that it wasn't uncommon for breeders to fight over results. They were really passionate! People today don't seem to have the same fire."

Kitako likes to anticipate, and look down the road—and she wonders if this is Morie's last dog show. Their old friend Masutaro Ito is still alive in Shimizu, but too old to come, like most of their longtime dog friends. Pretty soon, Kitako thinks, she and Morie will be too old to come. Or dead. Morie says if you worry too much about the future, you get distracted. But Kitako thinks if she considers the possibility that this may be the last show, she will appreciate it more. And so she does.

Being in Odate brings back memories. She can't help but miss Wataru. She remembers how he held court over the other dog boys and breeders, and sold his puppies as soon as they won first prize. She remembers hearing the news of Yamamoto, drinking too much and selling Happiness at the spring show—and then, how wonderful it was when she and Morie returned to Odate the following year with their new friends Mr. and Mrs. Ota. She remembers when the Akita

Preservation Museum was being built—just over the walking bridge from the park—and how the dog men of the north were asked to contribute their dog souvenirs and memorabilia. The glass display cases of the museum began filling up with beautiful old trophies and dog collars, Zen watercolors, postage stamps, and photographs of every champion Akita going back to 1931. Morie pledged so much money to the project—money they didn't have—that he and Kitako had to borrow against their pension. "My young life was really bound up or constricted by the policies of our government," she says, "and then after the war, it was tied up with dogs."

After the show, on the way back to Kurikoma, they drive by Castle No. 5 Town and drop in on Morie's sister, Haru. She is eighty but looks sixty, and the Dale Carnegie method is still working for her. She appears to own the entire town. The kimonos that she sells now are rare and expensive—thousands of dollars each—and her house and showroom are exquisite. But Haru's real passion is theater. She teaches *Nihon buyo,* the classic Japanese dance often seen on the Kabuki stage. Her daughter, Sachiko, teaches *biwa,* Japanese guitar.

Haru is devoted to *Nihon buyo.* Earlier in the year, she was awarded a lifetime achievement medal for her contribution to the arts in Akita prefecture—and she gave a performance in traditional makeup, wig, and elaborate kimono. She and Morie seem to have nothing in common while, at the same time, everything in common: Haru wants to talk mostly about *Nihon buyo* while Morie only cares to discuss dogs.

HE WAKES EARLY on the morning of May 22, 2006, Open Mountain Day, and sits on the big stone outside the glass doors to the bedroom. He looks at the garden. Its flowers peaked one week before, as they do almost every year, but still, eight days later, the hedge of azaleas below him is ablaze with brilliant pinks and purples and reds, and an almost electric green. "It took thirty-five years for the garden to mature," he says. "I am happy to have lived long enough to see it."

The strong morning sun shines on him. Shiro is howling. He smells Morie, or has heard him, and wants to see him. He was taken for a run earlier in the morning by Noritsugu but they didn't really open Mount Kurikoma together. Shiro hasn't done that since Morie had to stop in 2004. He is fifteen, and Morie is turning ninety. Even though they can't go up the mountain paths together, they are still a team. Wherever Morie goes, the dogs travel with him—dog memories, dog dreams, dog spirits.

He picks up a heavy stick—like a javelin—and begins his judo workout. He misses hiking, and the physical exercise of walking the paths. He used to travel ten thousand paces an hour until he was eighty-eight, then it was five thousand. The last year, it got down to three thousand—a pretty dismal number, except Morie is content to be able to walk at all.

He wonders how many hikers have gotten to the top of the mountain pass, to the wall of snow. He can see it in his mind's eye, so white. It seems to be waiting there for him.

Ryoko called the night before and spoke to Kitako. Ryoko has been treating Shiro for cancer, testing his blood, administering chemotherapy. Shiro's an old dog and bound to get something. Morie has let Ryoko handle everything and doesn't get involved, except to say that he doesn't want her to take the old dog to her hospital and keep it alive with feeding tubes. While on the subject, he made Kitako promise that if he got ill at home she wouldn't allow him to be taken to the hospital either. "No tubes going in and out of my body." If Shiro goes, he said, it might be time for him too.

. . .

MORIE AND KITAKO are popular with the grandchildren. They come on the bullet train with friends who marvel at the mountain, the fresh air and fresh food, and wonder what their lives must have been like. Morie and Kitako are open—and don't try to make things sound sweeter than they were.

"My grandfather told me that he didn't think about how hard it would be for my grandmother, living in the middle of nowhere without gas or electricity, because she was a city girl," says Masako, who lives in Houston and does research in medical microbiology at Texas A&M University. "For my grandmother's generation, living in the mountains was half-nightmare. It may have been a beautiful place, but these women did all the housework, cooking and cleaning, and laundry without a washing machine. For my grandfather, it was a dream. He was enjoying nature all day."

Ryoko calls often, and checks in on her father and mother and Shiro. Holidays and other occasions bring Moritake from Oyama City. Twice a year, when the weather and the garden are peaking, Mamoru arrives from New York, where he has been working at Bumble and bumble for thirteen years now. But Kurikoma pulls at him. He has made arrangements to buy the guesthouse and part of the property from his parents. "It took me a long time to understand how special it is here," he says. "Before that I was, you know, distracted."

The snow begins falling in the middle of December. It's called the snow country, or *Yukiguni*, because of its heavy accumulation. At the time of the full moon in February, there's a winter festival when the children make igloos out of bricks of ice and sleep overnight in them. In March, the valley begins to flood with snowmelt. In April, the new bamboo shoots can be picked in the forest and garden and eaten. Soon afterward the small slim cucumbers ripen in the greenhouse and Kitako serves them with a sesame dipping sauce.

Open Mountain Day comes in the third week of May. It started as a practice of farmers in the north, a part of *sangaku shinko,* mountain worship. The mountains were considered sacred—*kami* or nature deities lived there—and villagers made a pilgrimage to the summit as soon as the paths were passable in spring to pray for a peaceful year and a good harvest.

It's still one of Kitako's favorite days of the year, even if she and Morie don't make the journey anymore. She likes to remember how they used to wake early, when it was still dark. She'd stay in bed awhile and hear Morie outside rattling around in the kennels, the dogs getting excited, jumping on the fences, barking joyfully at the sight of Morie. When they arrived at the trailhead in the red pickup, the dogs were always so exuberant, so buoyant. They jumped out and sniffed every corner of the pathway, as if inhaling spring itself, their tails wagging and wagging. It was always still dark when she and Morie reached the end of the trail, where the plows had stopped and the wild mountain world began.

Facing the wall of white snow, Morie would ask her for the can of spray paint. She carried it in her pocket sometimes. She smiles to herself as she remembers how he'd write *Banzai Akita dogs* five feet high in the snow:

万 歳 秋 田 犬

Hurray, you beautiful dogs. Hurray!

ACKNOWLEDGMENTS

I would like to thank Morie and Kitako Sawataishi, who put up with my visits, my questions, and my appetite with unfailing grace and generosity. There were many long days and nights of talking around the dining table, many cups of green tea and snow country sake, and many plates of delicious surprises, thanks to Atsuko Fukushima. When I needed photographs scanned from Morie's old albums or a ride to a dog show, Noritsugu Fukushima came to my rescue. When I needed a fact checked or a family member tracked down, Mamoru Sawataishi was always cheerfully there. This book would not have been possible without him.

Akiko Kashiwagi took time away from her duties at *Newsweek* magazine to accompany me to Kurikoma as a combination translator, guide, and cultural ambassador. She was fun, lively, tireless—she even jogged around the Kurikoma reservoir—and endeared herself to the Sawataishis as well as to me. In Gojome-machi, Haru Ohara and her daughter, Sachiko Shimosaka, were generous with their time and *kiritampo*. In Tokyo, Mitsuko Otomo and her daughter, Yoko Kurihara, were encouraging and insightful. I am still thinking of the Night of the Giant Clam. Thank you.

Old friends Clay Chandler and Kyoko Altman came through, as they always do. Yukiko Altman generously put me up and made me laugh. In Kamakura, Jun and Keiko Sasano were endlessly fun and supportive. I want to thank Ruri Kawashima and Betty Borden at the Japan Society of New York for their many kindnesses over the years. And I am deeply grateful to Peter Grilli of the Japan Society of Boston for his enthusiasm, guidance, friendship, and astonishing expertise.

Terry Gallagher provided translation assists, cultural observations, and eagle-eyed copyediting help, and adeptly synopsized Yasufusa Hata-keyama's book, *Good Dogs, Good Life*, an invaluable introduction to the retirement life and mountain world of the Sawataishis. Jonathan Rausch gave me his copy of the definitive (and beguiling) *Japan: An Illustrated Encyclopedia*.

Other books came to my aid. John W. Dower's *Embracing Defeat*, a stunning historical account of life in postwar Japan, was an indispensable resource. Yasunari Kawabata's superb novel, *Snow Country*, took me to a place that I tried to describe as well as Kawabata but, of course, couldn't. Dogwise, I leaned on the works of behavioral scientist Stanley Coren (*How Dogs Think*, among others) and Temple Grandin's *Animals in Translation*. There are many good manuals specifically about raising Akitas, but for pure history, primary sources, and translations of Akita Preservation Society journal articles and oral histories, I am indebted to the Web site northlandakitas.com, *Japanese Dogs* by Michiko Chiba, and *Pawprints in Japan* by Nicholas C. Rhoden.

The dog world is big place, but Daisy Okas at the American Kennel Club provided contacts and research that made it seem smaller. In Odate, the Akita Preservation Society (AKIHO) and its museum gave me facts, figures, ideas, and inspiration.

Here at home I was encouraged by my husband, Bill, my son, William, my sister, Anina, my cousin Leslee and my mother, Peggy—a lifelong lover of animals and all things Japanese. My friend and agent, Flip Brophy at Sterling Lord Literistic, was wise, supportive, and practical, as always, as were her assistants, Sharon Skettini and Ruby Cramer.

At The Penguin Press, I'd like to thank Liza Darnton, Lindsay Whalen, and Darren Haggar. To my loyal editor and publisher, Ann Godoff: This book began and ends with you.

Anne Ghory-Goodman

Martha Sherrill is a former *Washington Post* staff writer known for her penetrating profiles of people, both famous and obscure. Her award-winning writing has appeared in *Esquire* and *Vanity Fair*, among other publications. She is the author of *The Buddha from Brooklyn*, a work of nonfiction, and two novels, *My Last Movie Star* and *The Ruins of California*. She lives in Massachusetts with her husband and son.

T65.1208